# let's
# cook
# DUTCH

# let's cook DUTCH

A Complete Guide
for the Dutch Oven Chef

Robert L. Ririe

ISBN: 0-88290-120-6
Library of Congress Number: 79-89360
Horizon Publishers' Catalog & Order Number: 4020

Printing:  11  12  13  14  15  16  17  18  19  20

Printed and distributed
in the United States of America by

 Horizon
Publishers
& Distributors, Incorporated
50 South 500 West   P.O. Box 490
Bountiful, Utah 84010-0490

# DEDICATION

This book is dedicated to a dear friend,
Dale Rogers,
with whom I shared many great cookouts.
He is gone, but not forgotten.
And to my wife and daughters;
without their help and encouragement,
this book would never have been completed.

For a backyard cookout or a camping treat, Dutch oven cooking is the way to good eating! Stack several ovens together and prepare your full menu at the same time.

# TABLE OF CONTENTS

## Part I
### Dutch Oven Cooking

## Part 2
### Dutch Oven Recipes

8

Dutch ovens are versatile! Use them for making your favorite pizza, preparing delicious pie crusts, or baking bread.

# INTRODUCTION

After using Dutch ovens for the last thirty years or so, and having given instructions and advice to numerous beginners, I began to look for a book that would tell the novice, step by step, how to take care of, and use, their Dutch ovens. I came to the conclusion that if I wanted a book like I was looking for, I would have to write it. I have attempted to explain how to cook in your Dutch oven so you will enjoy many good meals out of them and also to tell you how to care for your ovens so you will get many years of good use out of them.

Cooking outdoors in a Dutch oven can be an enjoyable experience. About the only thing better is eating what you've cooked. Anything tastes better when cooked in a Dutch oven and you don't have to be out in the wilds to do it. Almost everyone has some spot in their backyard that can be used. For years we used a bare spot in our backyard, where the grass didn't want to grow, as our Dutch oven spot. Just recently we had a barbeque built in and had a special place made to fit our Dutch ovens. We have turned out some terrific meals in both situations.

Whether the meals are for your own family or a group of friends, you will really enjoy this way of cooking. Once you are hooked on it, you will be trying to find excuses to use your Dutch oven continually.

When we have a group over for a cookout, everyone comes in carrying a Dutch oven. Try it! You'll have great companionship while everything is cooking, and excellent food when it's done—a terrific combination.

Another reason for this book is to point out all the variety of foods you can cook in Dutch ovens. When I was growing up, the only foods I had ever tried had been chicken and peach cobbler. I still like these two dishes, but I've discovered there are a great many other dishes that can be cooked and enjoyed. I like to try out new dishes all of the time. I haven't lost a food sampler yet, and the dishes have been mighty tasty. So don't be afraid to try; before long you'll be thinking up ideas of your own.

Cooking in Dutch ovens will take a little more time and effort than it would at home in the kitchen with all the electrical appliances that spoil us. I think though, that after you get the fundamentals down, you will enjoy the food more. I have never tasted anything that didn't taste better cooked outdoors in a Dutch oven. It will also give you time to enjoy nature and good friends while the food cooks. A little slower pace now and then is a good change from our daily routine.

Before you turn to the recipes, I hope you will take the time to read the part on the selection, care, use and other information about Dutch ovens. If you follow it carefully, you will be an old hand at Dutch oven cooking in no time, and I believe you will enjoy it as much as we do.

In the recipes I have suggested using some canned and packaged items, mainly because that is the easiest way to do Dutch oven cooking while you are camping. It's much more convenient than cooking from scratch. However, don't let me stop you from trying out your special sauces and cakes in your backyard. You just might have a winner!

As you become more proficient at Dutch oven cooking, you'll become increasingly aware of how versatile and useful a Dutch oven really is. If your power and gas were off for a long period of time, how would you feed yourself and family? Why not keep a few sacks of briquettes around and have a couple of Dutch ovens handy, and know how to use them.

For example, take the lid off your 14" oven, turn it over, level it on three rocks, and have a griddle for bacon and eggs, hot cakes, French toast or whatever you need, and it won't get your kitchen frying pan dirty. You will see that it gives the food a good flavor too. Wouldn't that be better than cold cereal and warm milk?

Anything that can be fried, boiled or baked, can be cooked in a Dutch oven. Most of these recipes I developed out deer hunting and fishing and have used them over the years. I hope you will get some good ideas and want to try them out. Don't be afraid to try things after you learn the basics. A group of us still go to Zion Park every year over Memorial weekend and a lot of cooking is done in Dutch ovens. I think that's why we enjoy going there—we all like to try out new things on each other.

May I suggest for a different party you have a Dutch oven pot luck. Have everyone bring their favorite dish, with ingredients enough to feed several, and their Dutch ovens. Have a place prepared so everyone can cook together. We have a place set aside next to our barbecue pit for large groups. When all the food is done, line up the Dutch ovens and everyone gets to try all of the various dishes. I'm sure you will have many good comments about the food. It is always a special time and we try to have several such parties each year. Why not try it yourself.

If I can be of help in planning it, or if you need a Dutch oven, 10", 12", or 14", write a note to Ririe Enterprises, c/o Bob Ririe, 105 Mallard Street, Las Vegas, Nevada 89107. Tell me what you need—prices on the ovens, or help in planning a group cookout. Make sure you include your name, address, and phone number. I will call or mail you the prices or information needed.

Also, if you have a good recipe that you have developed for Dutch oven use that was not in this book, please share it with me and I will assemble them in a special edition of favorite Dutch oven recipes.

Good fun and eating to all!

# Part 1

# Dutch Oven Cooking

You'll want a good set
of barbecue utensils.

A burlap bag is handy for
cleaning your Dutch oven.

A homemade hook is handy
for lifting hot oven lids.

# Chapter One

# The How and Whys of Dutch Oven Cooking

Dutch ovens are made of cast iron. Because they are so heavy, they heat evenly with little heat. The heavy lid, when it is set on properly, acts as a pressure cooker.

In pioneer days the Dutch oven was a mainstay for the people as they came across the plains. So many different foods could be cooked in these versatile kettles that they were really a prized possession. I can imagine, when some of the companies had to lighten their load on the way, that they would have been very reluctant to give up their Dutch ovens.

In case of a power failure, a Dutch oven would be a good item to have on hand. I have prepared meals this way when the power was off for a couple of hours and we were unable to cook any other way. We had a delicious meal and the Dutch oven saved the day.

**How to "Season" a New Dutch Oven**

After acquiring your Dutch oven you should "season" it to prepare it for use. The manufacturers of Dutch ovens put a protective coating on the inside of the kettles. This must be removed before cooking in them.

Place the Dutch oven over heat until it becomes quite warm. Then wipe the bottom and sides briskly with paper towels until the towels come out clean. After this protective coating is removed, pour a small quantity of vegetable oil in the pan. Wipe the sides and bottom again with paper towels, spreading the oil completely over the whole surface. Don't leave much oil in the pan, just a light surface covering. If you leave too much oil, it has a tendency to become rancid. Wipe

the lid with oil, too. You would do well to coat the top side of
the lid and the outside of the oven with oil, too. Just use the
oily paper towels you wiped the inside with—you don't need
much. This helps keep your lid and oven looking better, and
helps it to resist rust.

Now your Dutch oven is ready to use.

## How to Re-season an Oven

If you haven't used your Dutch oven in a very long time,
or if the oil in it has gone rancid (you can tell by the smell when
you go to use it), or if it has lost its season through lack of care,
then start all over again just as if it were a new one. Heat it,
wipe it out, and then re-oil it. Wipe it out again as explained
in the previous section, leaving only a light covering.

If your Dutch oven should become rusty, all is not lost.
In most cases it can be saved and used again. Wipe off all the
rust you can, then warm your oven up and start cleaning it
with oil. Rub it especially well where it is rusty. It may take
a little time, but if you can use your oven again, it's worth it.

If your oven has been put away dirty and left for a long
period of time, the insides may have become pitted. An oven in
this condition can be saved, too. Scour it with a soap pad,
rinse out the soap, heat until the moisture is completely out,
then oil it as described before.

## Selecting the Right Size Dutch Oven

Dutch ovens come in a range of sizes from the small 8" to
the large 16". Occasionally you will come across one that is
extra deep but usually the depth is a standard size.

Some of you may have a Dutch oven that was given to
you, or one that you fell heir to. If it's a 12" or 14", you are
lucky; these sizes are good for almost everything you'll want to
cook, even it it's only for two or three people. There have been
times when all I had with me was my 14" oven and I wanted to
cook for just my wife and myself. It works out fine.

If you are only going to buy one Dutch oven, I would
suggest a 14" size. Certainly you should not choose one
smaller than a 12". You can always put smaller amounts of
food in a larger pan, but if you are cooking for a group, it's

hard to make a small oven stretch to accommodate all you want to cook.

The following is a chart telling how much each oven holds, and suggesting the types of foods I've cooked in them:

| Oven Size | Oven Capacity | Types of Foods Cooked |
|---|---|---|
| 8" | 2 qts | vegetables, baked beans |
| 10" | 4 qts | baked bread; baked beans; rolls; small cobbler |
| 12" | 6 qts | main dishes to serve 12-14 people; cobbler |
| 14" | 8 qts | main dishes to serve 16-20 people; cobbler |
| *16" | 12 qts | any large group dish will serve 22-26 |

*No longer made. If you have one, you're lucky!

## How to Clean Your Dutch Oven

I always try to get my Dutch oven cleaned as soon as we are through eating the meal prepared in it. There is usually enough heat left at this time to reheat the oven for cleaning, and heat is an important factor in cleaning the ovens.

Another reason I like to clean it at this time is that then I know it's clean if I want to use it again the same day.

Place your oven over heat and scrape all the food from the Dutch oven with a spatula or a putty knife (see secton on tools) until the sides and bottom are as clean as possible. Then, with a paper towel and spatula lift out the loose particles. Continue to scrape and wipe until it is as clean as you can get it. Pour in a little vegetable oil, wipe out the excess, and be sure to coat the sides and bottom. Wipe off any moisture that has accumulated on the lid, and wipe it with oil also.

A good item to have for cleaning your oven is a burlap bag. Just scrape out your oven with a spatula or putty knife and then wipe it good with the burlap bag. This is faster than paper towels, as it won't tear like the towels do. After it is clean, wipe the oil all over it with a paper towel. Apply just a light coating, and it will be ready for the next time you want to use it. When the burlap bag gets too dirty, you can wash it and have a clean bag to use.

I don't recommend washing a Dutch oven, but if it gets to the point where you feel the only way it will come clean is by washing, then go ahead. Just remember—don't put ice cold water in a hot Dutch oven, or pour hot water in a very cold one—it can cause it to break. After the oven has been washed, heat it thoroughly for several minutes to remove all the moisture. Then the oven must be re-seasoned with oil.

Some who own Dutch ovens like to burn them out to get them clean, by putting them upside down in the fire to burn out all the leftover food. I don't recommend burning them out. Though it gets the oven clean, it also takes the seasoning out of the oven, and that is what gives the food the flavor. After ovens are burned out they have to be re-seasoned, and they must be cooked in several times to put the flavor back in. The longer and more you use them, the better the flavor gets. I have one 14" oven that has been used by me for over 20 years and has never been burned out. The food from it is always better than my other ovens. I would part with one of the others that are much newer before I would part with this old one.

Try cleaning your oven the various ways I've explained and decide which is the best way for you. Keep in mind, if you take good care of your Dutch ovens, they will take good care of you for many good times and good meals.

## Tools for Dutch Oven Cooking

There are several tools or aids that will make your Dutch oven cooking much easier. Long-handled barbecue utensils are handy if you don't want to get too close to the fire. These include long-handled tongs, a spatula, and a fork. I have two pair of tongs, one for moving the briquets and coals around, the other for picking up food such as chicken and ribs. You can use a fork, but remember every time you stick the fork in the meat you are cooking, you lose some of the juices.

A long-handled hook is a good item to have also. This is used for lifting the lid of the Dutch oven to check your food and for

A single hook.

lifting the whole oven to check on or replace coals. There are several kinds of hooks I have used, and all of them are homemade. You'll need two separate hooks.

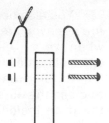

    To make your own set of hooks, use a shovel handle and two tie-down hooks, 5/16" x 3-1/2" size. Cut the shovel handle in half and drill two holes in one end of each half. Mount the hooks to the handle with two bolts just long enough to reach through the nuts.

    If you are handy with tools and have welding equipment available, you can use two hooks for each handle, one on each side. Weld a piece of reinforcing rod on one of the hooks. It will steady the Dutch oven lid when it is being removed.

    You can also make a useful hook from a sprinkler system metal turn-on handle. Just bend the end with the two prongs in a 45⁰ angle and it will hold the lids level, but not as good as the other hooks do. If it is too long for you, cut it off to fit your needs.

A double hook.

A hook made from a sprinkler turn-on handle.

    A 2" to 3" putty knife, the kind you can buy in any hardware store, is another tool I use a lot. This makes a convenient scraper when I am cleaning my oven. It's a little easier to use one of these than an awkward long-handled spatula. And as I mentioned in the cleaning section, it takes a lot of scraping to get an oven clean.

You also need a shovel to transfer coals and to cover your fire after you are through with it. I carry a short-handled shovel when we are out camping, but use a regular garden shovel when at home in our backyard.

Dutch ovens get smoky on the outside. If you don't want to clean the outside, find a box that will hold it snugly and put the oven inside the box so the soot won't rub off on your clothes, equipment, and car. Some people put their Dutch ovens into a burlap bag before putting it into the box.

You'll need something clean and flat to set your oven lid on during cooking. A large board, several inches longer than the diameter of the lid, serves this purpose very well.

**Build a Dutch Oven Pit**

If you have a barbecue built in your backyard or are going to build one later on, and enjoy Dutch oven cooking, why not add a Dutch oven pit to the side of your barbecue? It works very well and you can stand up to cook. I designed one for our backyard. (See illustration below.) It works so well, I'll give you the details and you can build one yourself.

Add a Dutch oven pit to your home barbecue area.

It is 88" long, 41" high, and 36½" wide. The Dutch oven pit is lined with a layer of fire bricks. It is 24" wide, by 33" long, and

10" deep, and will hold two ovens. You can fit a regular barbecue on the other end. The two compartments in the bottom
can be used to store extra briquettes. Keep a good supply on
hand and rotate them to use the old ones first. You can also
keep the tools you use all the time for cooking in there.

**Building Fires for Dutch Oven Cooking**

I am going to cover two kinds of cooking fires in this
section. Both are equally good for Dutch oven cooking, but
which you use will depend on where you are.

*1  WOOD FIRE—Suggested for use when camping.*

It's important when you use a wood fire to have two
separate fires. One is for the Dutch oven to cook on, the other
is to produce new coals. The fire for the coals has to be replen-
ished with wood continually. The wood will burn down to
coals, which in turn are removed with a shovel and placed on
the Dutch oven fire as needed.

Place rocks around an area where you plan to make your
large coal fire. Dig a shallow pit into which the coals will be
allowed to fall. This makes it easier to shovel them out to use.
Start this fire about ½ hour before you plan to start cooking.
Don't use large logs—you want your fire to burn down to coals
quickly and large logs take too long. When your fire burns
down to where you have nice hot coals, you are ready to start
your cooking. Remove what you need with a shovel. Remember

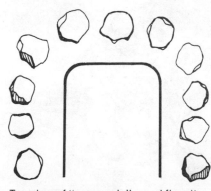
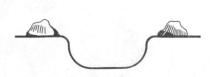

Top view of "new coals" wood fire pit.    Side view of "new coals" wood fire pit.

to keep replenishing the fire so you will have coals throughout your cooking time. These coals do not burn as long as briquets so you must keep replacing them on your cooking fire throughout the cooking time. It takes a lot of wood to keep a Dutch oven going for any length of time (see Figures 1 and 2), so unless you have a good supply of wood and are in an area where fires are allowed, I suggest you use method #2, Charcoal Briquets.

*2. CHARCOAL BRIQUETS—Suggested for backyard cooking and fire hazard area.*

I always use briquets when available because they are almost smokeless, more convenient, and the heat from them can be controlled better than with wood coals. Just a reminder—don't ever use them indoors as they give off a toxic gas.

As with the wood fire, you should have two fires going. One should be kept going so you can replenish the cooking fire. About 30 to 45 minutes before you are ready to cook, start your briquets. Use as hard a surface as possible, because soft ground or sand will smother them. Stack your unlit briquets in a mound. Pour lighter fluid or charcoal fire starter fluid, not gas, over them. If you think they are going out, fan them. This will usually bring life back to them. If fanning them doesn't help, pour more lighter fluid on and light again.

Pile unlit charcoal mound before lighting.

When the briquets are red hot, they are usually an ashy grey and flare red when fanned. If you are still in doubt, hold your hand a few inches over the briquets. If they are burning, you'll know by the heat they are giving out.

As you take away the briquets for use, pile additional unlighted ones on one side of the pile. These will light from the starter pile and you will always have briquets burning as you need them.

If cooking for a large group, you'll need a lot of briquets so make a large pile. But only pour the lighter fluid over what you need to start cooking with. The other hot ones will start the briquets close by. You can remove them as needed. Keep adding more briquets to the pile.

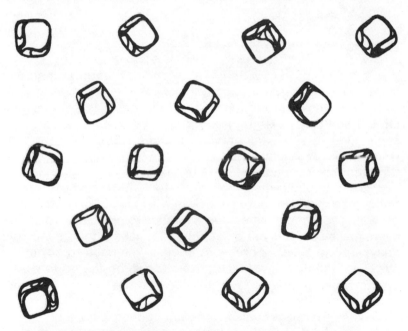

Lay the burning charcoals flat in a checkerboard pattern.

You can judge how many to start at a time by how many ovens you are using. It takes 16 to 18 briquets for the bottom of a 14" oven to keep it cooking well for frying or roasting. An additional 12 or so are needed on top. After they are burning well, put them in a checkerboard pattern, flat side up, to get the most heat from them. Don't put them on edge—that provides a much smaller area of heat. You can soon tell if the heat is too much or not enough when you check the food you are cooking. Notice how the food is doing, then add a few briquets if needed, or remove some if fire is too hot.

When fixing a fire for baking of cobblers, upside down cake, cake, cookies, pie, etc., most of the heat must be on top so you will use a checkerboard patter on the bottom of only 6 or 8 briquets and 18 to 24 on top in a circle pattern.

The circle pattern is a good one for baking because sometimes a section of the item you're baking won't be cooking evenly so you can push briquets to where they're needed or remove some where the food is cooking too rapidly. Use the long-handled tongs and shovel to add the briquets or remove them.

**Cooking With Your Dutch Oven**

After you have your coals ready, the next important step is to get your oven ready for cooking.

Your oven will function better if you get it as level as possible. I do this by placing rocks or bricks on two sides of the coals. Pour a small quantity of cooking oil in the oven and when the oven is placed on the bricks, the oil will indicate if the oven is level or not. More on this later.

When cooking meat, the first step will be to brown it on both sides by cooking it in the oven with the lid off. Then, after browning your meat, when you are ready to place the lid on the oven, make sure it is set on securely to make a good seal. This heavy lid will act as a pressure cooker when set on correctly. Now with the lid on, you can put hot coals on the lid to speed up the cooking time or to brown food on the top, such as biscuits and breads.

When there are coals on the lid, you must be very careful how you remove the lid to check your food. I have had a breeze hit the lid and blow coals into the oven (which you may guess does not help the food any). If the wind is blowing, shield the oven and lid from the wind with your body while opening the oven. Two hooks are handy to have when it comes to lifting the lid—one to lift and one to steady. Also when you have taken the lid off, be careful of where you set it down. Moisture from

Use fewer coals under the Dutch oven when baking cakes, cobblers, etc.

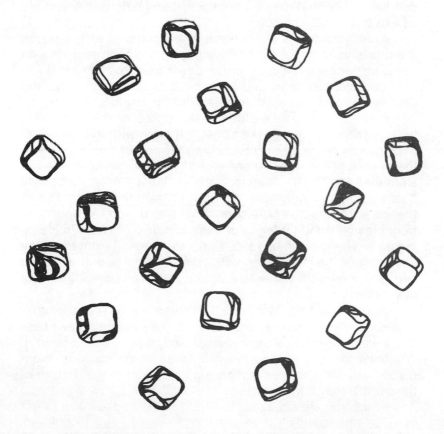

More briquets are needed on top for cobblers, cakes, pies, etc.

the oven will have collected on the underside of the lid. If you set it on the ground, it will pick up loose dirt. Decide on a place where the coals will not tip off and the underside will stay clean. A wide board or flat rock serves very well for this purpose.

If you are using more than one Dutch oven, you can save fuel by stacking them one on top of the other. This way the coals on the lid of one give heat to the bottom of the next. The only drawback to this is that you must remove the top Dutch ovens to check the bottom ones. But if you are willing to put up with a little inconvenience, it's an economical way to cook with several Dutch ovens.

I would like to go into more detail on some of the things that have been just mentioned. I feel it will help those that are new to Dutch oven cooking.

Aluminum foil is very useful when cooking with a Dutch oven. It is used as a help in cleaning up the oven and isn't an absolute necessity. If you want to use it as an oven lining, I will tell you how. The first step is to measure about 6" more foil than the oven is wide, then tear it off the roll. Lay it evenly inside of the oven and mold it to the shape of the oven carefully so you don't tear it. Then cut it off flush with the top of the oven by running a sharp knife along the top of the oven. Hold the excess foil in your other hand. If you are going to use the aluminum foil to lift out a yummy dish like a Pineapple Upside Down Cake, then don't cut it off but roll up all the extra foil to the top edge, inside of the oven. This way it won't keep the lid from closing tight. Lining your oven can be a big help in cleaning up as the foil can be folded up and removed from the oven and most of the mess goes with it. A quick wipe with a burlap bag, some oil on a paper towel, and the oven is ready for the next time.

Another fast tip. Most of the recipes for meat and poultry dishes call for ¼ cup of vegetable oil. I like bacon grease best and always save it in a separate can so I have it when I need it. Whatever oil you use will work fine. When cooking meat dishes and chicken, use just enough oil to cover the bottom of the oven. It may take as little as ¼ cup.

When you are checking the food being cooked, if it is not cooking hot enough (when you can't see or hear it cooking), then take your long-handled tongs and pat the briquets or coals. Sometimes the ash builds up and they all but go out. If you still can't see any red on them, add some more briquets to the bottom or top or both if they need it.

You can tell if your fire is too hot, when you check it, if it is sputtering and popping a great deal. To cool the fire, take the long tongs and remove some heat from the bottom and top. I usually take off about ¼ of the briquets. If there are eighteen on top, remove five of them, and if there are eight on the bottom, remove two. If the fire continues to be too hot, remove a fourth more of the coals so the food will simmer as you want it to.

When you move your oven from place to place, it is handy to use the long hooks. They will keep your hands away from the hot coals. If you don't have a hook yet, use hot pad gloves. They are also useful, and will save you from the hot handle so you can move the ovens and stack them as needed.

When removing the extra grease that you will have from time to time in your ovens, hold the oven by the wire handle with hot pad covered hand or a hook. Catch one of the legs with another hook and tip the oven. Pour the extra grease into a can. You can either save it or throw it out. This just saves people from getting burned.

You will want to take your Dutch ovens when you are going on a camping trip. I can tell you a couple of tips that will help get your oven there in good shape. The first way is to keep them in the boxes they came packed in. This can be done until the boxes are in no condition to hold them anymore. When this happens, you can make a box out of light plywood. Make it with a cover and handles to carry it with. Or, get some burlap bags to haul your ovens in. Either of these will keep the lids from banging around too much and help to keep the ovens clean. They will also keep any of the black from the ovens from getting on anything else. Remember, as I said before, if you take care of your ovens, they will take good care of you when you need them.

Another tip that can be a big help is putting your oven on two bricks or rocks. This will help make it level and keep the oven above the coals enough so that the coals won't smother. This allows the air to circulate over them and it will give you enough room to reach in to tap them for more heat or to remove or add briquets as needed.

Placing your oven on bricks allows air to circulate around the coals.

Use the Dutch oven lid as a convenient frying pan.

Another tip a lot of people don't think of is using your Dutch oven lid on two bricks as a griddle or frying pan. When we go on a fishing or hunting trip, all we usually take are the Dutch ovens and we do all the cooking in them. I had been doing it so long I thought everybody else did too. But from some of the looks and comments made, I found others hadn't discovered the convenience of cooking on the oven lid.

Here's how to do it. Put the bricks or rocks far enough apart to hold the outside edge of the lid. Turn it upside down, so the ring that is usually on the top to lift it is now on the bottom. Keep it as level as you can and close enough to the coals to get the heat, just make sure that you don't smother the coals. When the lid gets warm, you can cook whatever you want on it, just like a frying pan. You can put two lids side by side and cook hot cakes or French toast on one and eggs and bacon on the other. I think you will be surprised at how well it works. It adds flavor to the food even though it is only the lid that is being used.

If you're cooking for a large group and you don't have enough ovens, use the regular ovens as frying pans and take off all the lids and use them too. It will double your cooking utensils and speed up the meal.

## Remember the Basics of Fire Safety

In this section on how to build a fire for Dutch oven cooking, it's appropriate to say a few words about safety and warn you about some of the particular dangers associated with this type of cookery.

First, when cooking with charcoal briquets, don't ever take the briquets indoors to cook with or to warm up your tent, camper, motor home, etc. They give off a toxic gas and it can kill if confined in an enclosed area. There are several killed every year by briquets used in closed campers. If you are cooking and it starts to rain or snow, put a tarp or an umbrella over you until you are finished cooking. You can eat inside, but leave the coals outside where they can't hurt anyone.

Second, when cooking outside and the briquets are not in a barbecue or Dutch oven pit, you must be careful of the hot briquets lying around on the ground. The more people you have cooking, the more careful you should be because the briquets are very hot and will give anyone that picks them up in their bare hands a bad burn. Young children seem to be curious about them. I have seen them pick up a whole handful in a matter of a few seconds when they slip in by the cooking fires before anyone had a chance to stop them and they got a nasty burn. To keep this from happening, always try to keep the kids busy somewhere away from the cooking area, and leave someone to make sure that they don't walk in. The ovens are hot enough to burn them too, so keeping the kids out will keep them from falling on a hot oven or in a fire.

Third, when you are doing the cooking always use the tools, like hooks, etc. for handling the ovens. Use the tongs and shovel for handling the briquets, so you don't get a bad burn.

You must always be careful of where you stand when doing the cooking because with the synthetic material shoes are made of now, you can melt your shoes off your feet before you realize it. I have seen several burns this way and a few pairs of shoes ruined. A simple rule is: when you are through cooking on a fire and the oven has been removed, take *all* the briquets or coals away from the spot you are through with. Use them in another spot to cook with, or put them back in the main fire, to be used later. Then shovel the spot over so it won't burn anyone. You can save somebody from burning their shoes or worse.

I don't want you to get the idea that Dutch oven cooking is particularly dangerous, however. In all the years I have been cooking, I have never had a bad burn because I am careful and use the tools to do what must be done. I have seen others get burned, though, and it can sure cut a camping trip short to run somebody in to be treated at a first aid center for something that didn't need to happen.

So be careful and watch your kids and the location of the cooking fires. Use the tools to do the job and you will have many good times with your Dutch ovens.

Every once in a while when we have planned a Dutch oven cookout, the weather turns nasty. Then we have two alternatives. First, you can cancel (which no one likes, especially if your company is visiting from out of town and all you've talked about since they carried their bags in and got settled, was the Dutch oven meal you were going to prepare for them). The other choice is cooking over the burners on the kitchen stove, or in the oven. I used both of these indoor methods the last time this happened.

When cooking on the stove or in the oven, you must remember to check your heat more often than when cooking outdoors. In outside cooking, briquets and ashes burn down and so you must replenish them. But indoors, the gas flame or electricity remains constant so you must adjust the heat to the needs of the item you are cooking.

You will find when you place the Dutch oven over the burner, the legs will fit around it and the bottom of the oven will not touch the burner. It's sort of like outside when you set the oven on bricks so it doesn't rest on the briquets.

Turn on the heat and proceed as if you were outside, but just remember to watch and regulate the heat.

I'll go through step by step one of the meals I've prepared indoors to give you an idea of how it's done. I know most of you don't need me from this point on, especially if you've done a lot of Dutch oven cooking, but for the less brave, just follow along with me.

I placed a 14" Dutch oven over the 8" burner, set the heat at medium high and added 4 tablespoons bacon grease. When it was hot, I put in a 6 lb. boneless brisket and browned it well on both sides, seasoning to taste. When the roast was as browned as I liked it, I put on the lid and let it simmer. I turned the heat down to medium. I let it simmer about 30 minutes, checking it often and turning the brisket every few minutes so it cooked evenly on both sides. Approximately one hour later I added two 4 oz. cans of sliced mushrooms and two cans of mushroom soup. This made the sauce. I then let it continue to cook at medium heat until tender.

*Note:* This could be cooked in the oven too, if you wanted. Brown as above and set the oven to 350°, cook it until tender—about two hours for a 6-lb. brisket.

After I had the brisket well on its way, I started the potatoes and onions. I placed another 14" Dutch oven over another burner at medium high heat. I cut the strips of 1 pound of bacon into five sections. (This cooked up into bite-size pieces and mixed well with the onions and potatoes.) While the bacon was cooking, I finished preparing the potatoes and onions. I sliced the potatoes about 1/8" thick and cut the onions in quarters. When the bacon was crisp, I added the other ingredients, turned the heat to medium and let them cook. I was careful to keep a close watch and when turning these, I got clear down to the bottom of the oven to turn everything over.

In another 14" oven, I started the pineapple upside down cake. I lined the pan with heavy duty aluminum foil. I put one square of butter in the Dutch oven over medium high heat. Then I removed it from the heat, and added the brown sugar, nuts, and pineapple in the bottom of the Dutch oven. I put the cake in the oven to cook at 350°, without a lid on it. It cooked in about 35 to 45 minutes. I tested it as with all cakes.

Now back to the roast. When the roast was done, as tender as I wanted it, I took it from the Dutch oven, placed it on the cutting board and sliced it into serving slices (remembering to always slice the meat across the grain). Then I placed it back in the sauce and let it simmer for a few minutes longer.

When the potatoes and onions became tender, we were ready to eat.

You may think it is silly to cook indoors with Dutch ovens, but it gives it that extra special flavor Dutch oven cooking has and it's really not that much trouble.

I remember one fishing trip I was on when it rained a great deal. We got out the Coleman stove, placed it on a table, put a tarp over us, and cooked many good meals this way in the Dutch ovens. So don't let inclement weather keep you from having a Dutch oven cookout, or rather a "cook-in." Try it some time. Good luck!

# Part 2

# Dutch Oven Recipes

What could be better
than Beef Brisket?

Use an aluminum
foil liner when baking
a cake in your
Dutch oven.

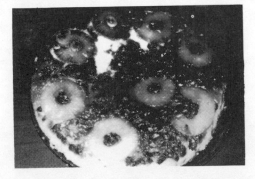

Pineapple-upside-down
cake is one of the
author's Dutch
oven favorites.

# Chapter Two

# Sauces

Rather than beginning with the meat dishes, let me first suggest a few simple sauces to use with the meats that will add zest to any meal. Most of the sauces I will be mentioning in the recipes are based on canned soups. Since my decision to start using these as my sauces, I have found that they are easier to transport on a cookout, and that they are much more convenient than taking all of the ingredients needed and starting from scratch. Shop around; try different brands. I have my favorite, and I am sure you will find yours. Of course, if you are one of the die-hards who insists on making your own sauces, then more power to you. I'm sure they will turn out just as well.

## Mushroom Sauce - Onion Sauce - Tomato Sauce - Cheese Sauce

To one can of creamed soup, add ½ can of canned milk to slightly thin the soup. Pour this over your meat or vegetables. If you want the sauce to be the consistency of gravy, add more milk. On some of the meats I cook I put the soup in as is, straight from the can. The juice from the meat thins the soup out enough. This also gives it a very good flavor. You will have to do a little bit of experimenting to find out how you like it best.

Just use your favorite canned soup.

## Teriyaki Sauce

This has always been one of my favorite sauces. I use this to marinate meat dishes. Until the time I decided to write this recipe book, I had always made it with a pinch of this and a "glug, glug" of that; but writing down the recipe requires more precision. The following is a very good marinating sauce:

> 1 12-oz. bottle teriyaki
> 1 4-oz. bottle Hickory Smoked Bar-B-Que sauce
> 1 Tbsp. Liquid Smoke
> 1 Tsp. Worcestershire Sauce

Blend all ingredients together. Pour over your meat and let stand at least one hour.

Use some of this mixture as the moisture with which to cook your meat. The flavor increases the longer it cooks, so test it often.

# Bar-B-Que Sauce

I think almost everyone has a favorite barbecue sauce recipe; but, in case you are looking for one, use the following:

> 1 15-oz. can tomato sauce
> ½ cup brown sugar
> 1 Tbsp. vinegar
> ½ Tsp. prepared mustard
> *Optional:* 3 or 4 pieces crisp bacon crumbled
> 1 Tbsp. dehydrated onion flakes
> 1 Tsp. Liquid Smoke (for smoky flavor)

When we are out camping, I use a prepared sauce. It's easier to transport it and after trying several I have found one that meets the qualifications I want in a Hickory Flavor Bar-B-Que sauce. I suggest that you try several and buy your favorite brand.

# Chapter Three

# Meat Dishes

## Beef in Gravy

Select any roast you want for this dish. You don't need a quality cut—just choose the roast that is the best buy. When you are through with it, it will taste like a choice cut.

Figure ½ pound for each adult and ¼ pound for each child.

Place the oven over the heat. Make sure it is as level as possible. Salt and pepper to taste. Cover with water. Bring to a boil, then simmer until tender (approximately 1½ hours for a medium-sized roast).

When roast is tender, transfer it to the cutting board. Remove fat and bones, then slice meat into serving pieces.

Thicken the juice from the meat with flour (remove the oven from coals to do this—it will reduce chance of lumps forming). Return the oven to the heat, bring to boil and put cut pieces of roast in the gravy mixture. Let simmer 5 to 10 minutes.

Serve over rice or noodles.

If you have leftovers, think about having Dutch Mulligan Stew!

## Venison Combination Roast

| | |
|---|---|
| 12" to 14" Dutch oven | ¼ cup vegetable oil or bacon |
| 1 small venison roast (deer) | grease |
| 1 small pork roast | salt and pepper |

Some people do not like venison (deer meat); but, if the meat is taken care of properly, then aged, and if cooked right, it has a very good flavor. I have never had anyone refuse to eat it when it was cooked by me! This is one way to make it tasty; see if you don't agree.

Level the Dutch oven and pour in the vegetable oil. While it is heating up, salt and pepper both roasts. When the oven is hot, put the roasts in with tongs and brown them on all sides. Keep the lid on to keep in the juice, and heat the oven after the meat is brown on all sides. Add one cup of water to the Dutch oven and recover it, adding heat to the top. Remember to keep checking and turning the meat all the time so that all the sides have a chance to soak up the flavor and not dry out. After it has simmered for about 1 to 1½ hours, test it by using a fork to see if it's tender. If it's not, let it cook another 10 to 20 minutes, or until the fork goes in easily. I'll bet you will never have a better venison roast in your life. The pork will help flavor it and keep it from getting dry, and the venison will help flavor the pork roast. Use the juice as gravy over the meat. It will be good as is, or you can thicken with flour to use on potatoes. I'll bet you won't find a better gravy than this. You may want to add a little more salt and pepper for your own taste. It does make an excellent meat dish, and one that you will remember.

If there happens to be any of the venison left over or the juice, it will make good "Sloppy Joes" or Mulligan Stew, so keep it and try one of these recipes when you get the chance. They are both good.

# Flank Steak with Onion Sauce

flank steak
  ½-lb. per person (adult)
  ¼-lb. per child
salt, pepper, and Accent

can of cream of onion soup
¼ cup vegetable oil
1 cup milk

This steak has a good flavor. I use it a lot. It makes excellent Swiss steak, too. The recipe that is in this book is made with round steak because I wanted to show this one as a change.

First, trim extra fat and gristle off the steak, if any, then salt and papper and Accent to taste. When the Dutch oven is level, pour in the oil and when it is hot, add the steak. Brown it on both sides, then cover. Let simmer while you mix up the sauce. In a separate pan, put one can cream of onion soup. Add one cup milk. Stir until smooth, then take the lid off of the oven, and pour it over the steaks. Put on the lid and let the meat simmer until tender. Check every 15 minutes. It will take about 1 to 1½ hours, depending on how thick it was; but, it will be worth waiting for! You can use the sauce as a gravy over potatoes or rice. This cut of meat has an excellent flavor. Cooking it in a Dutch oven serves to make an excellent flavor even better.

When you are in a hurry for a quick meal, you can add canned new potatoes to this steak. I have done this and my guests didn't know it because the meat was so good and flavorful that it helped flavor even the canned potatoes. If you get in a hurry out fishing some time, try it; it's mighty good eating.

# Swiss Steak with Mushroom Sauce

| | |
|---|---|
| round steak | flour |
| ½-lb. per adult | salt, pepper, Accent |
| ¼-lb. per child | ¼ cup vegetable oil or |
| 1 can mushrooms | shortening |
| 1 can cream of mushroom soup | |

While your fire is getting ready, you can first prepare the steak by cutting off extra fat and gristle; then, salt and pepper to taste.

On your cutting board, sprinkle some flour on the round steak and pound it in with a butcher knife until it is well covered; then, turn the steak over, sprinkle the other side, and pound it until well covered. It is now ready for the Dutch oven.

Level your oven over the heat and pour in the oil. When hot, put in the steak and brown it on both sides. When all the steak is brown, then cover and simmer for at least ½ hour more while you prepare the mushroom sauce and mushrooms. If you like extra mushrooms as I do, now is the time to add them to the Dutch oven so they can brown before you add the sauce. Open the can, drain, and add as many as you like to the steak. Stir them in so they will be browning, then recover the oven.

To make your sauce, open 1 can cream of mushroom soup and pour it in a separate bowl. Add ½ can of milk and stir it up until smooth. After the mushrooms you just added have browned, pour the sauce over the steaks and cover it up again. You can add more heat on top for extra cooking speed as long as you keep checking the steaks to be sure that they don't cook dry.

Cook the steaks until tender to the fork (about 1½ hours, or 2), depending on the amount of steak and how tough the meat was.

When done, you can serve the sauce as a gravy for potatoes or rice; it has a very good flavor.

# Pork Bar-B-Que Ribs

pork back ribs
  2 to 3 per adult;
  1 to 2 per child
    *or*
rack regular ribs
  4 to 6 per adult;
  2 to 4 per child

Hickory barbecue sauce,
  1 to 2 bottles
½ cup vegetable oil or
  shortening

Here again, be selective. When you buy ribs, buy them with some meat on them. I prefer the back ribs; they have a lot more meat on them. Whichever one you buy, buy quality meat, as lean as you can find.

If you buy a rack of regular ribs, cut them in serving pieces so they can be browned and turned over a lot easier. The back ribs are already in pieces.

Level the oven on the heat and add the oil. When it's hot, brown the ribs on all sides, then cover to simmer for about 30 to 45 minutes, checking every 15 minutes to see how they are doing. Add oil if needed. Keep rotating the ribs so they will not burn on one side but will brown evenly.

After the 45 minutes, add the barbecue sauce to the ribs, then recover. Add more heat and continue to simmer, checking about every 15 minutes, mixing up the ribs in the sauce so that they will all get the flavor of the sauce.

Don't hurry them too fast. Most people rush these before they are done. Give them a chance to simmer until tender to the fork. It will take about 2 hours for a 14" Dutch oven full of back ribs to cook until tender, but they are sure worth the wait, and these will be as good eating as you have ever had.

# Beef Short Ribs

beef short ribs
  2 or 3 per person
¼ cup vegetable oil
salt and pepper and Accent

Hickory barbecue sauce
  (optional)
small new potatoes (4 per
  person)

Select a good lean cut of ribs so you will have some meat on them. If too fat, trim some of it off first while your Dutch oven is heating up with the oil in it.

Salt and pepper and Accent the ribs to taste, then put them in to brown. Brown on all sides, cover and simmer. After the ribs are all good and brown (45 minutes or so), add the new potatoes to the oven. Keep rotating the ribs and the potatoes so that all will get brown. The potatoes will soak up the flavor from the meat. Let simmer until tender. You can test with a fork; it will take 1½ to 2 hours to cook in a full 14" Dutch oven.

As an option, you can add barbecue sauce to the ribs instead of the new potatoes, when they are all browned. These are good, too, especially if you can't eat the pork ribs.

# Breaded Pork Chops

pork chops
  2 per person, 1 per child
¼ cup vegetable oil or
  shortening

salt, pepper, and Accent
¼ to ½ cup flour
12" to 14" Dutch oven

For breaded pork chops, I prefer to use the boneless loin chops; but, the other with the bone will be fine, too.

To start, trim off all the extra fat, then salt, pepper, and Accent to taste, then cover with flour, removing all the excess flour. They are now ready for the Dutch oven.

Level the oven. Pour in the oil and make sure it's hot, then put in the chops, brown on both sides, then cover. Add heat to the top and simmer until tender to the fork. It will take about 1 hour, depending on how thick the chops are cut and how much heat you use and how many you are cooking.

But they are sure good this way.

# Pork Chops with Mushroom Sauce

pork chops                          12" to 14" Dutch oven
  2 per person, 1 per child         1 can cream of mushroom soup
¼ cup vegetable oil or              ½ cup milk
  shortening                        1 can mushrooms (optional)
salt, pepper, and Accent

There are a lot of ways to fix pork chops and this is the other way I like them besides breaded. As in the breaded recipe, I prefer the boneless loin chops, but any kind will do and they all taste great.

First, trim off the extra fat, then salt, pepper and Accent to taste. You are now ready to put it in the Dutch oven.

Level the Dutch oven. Add oil. When hot, put in the pork chops to brown them. Turn to brown on all sides. When brown, add the can of mushrooms. This is optional; if you don't like mushrooms, don't put them in. If you do, put them in now to get them brown before the sauce is added. While these are browning, mix up the can of mushroom soup in a bowl and add the ½ cup milk. Stir until well mixed. When the pork chops are good and brown, and the mushrooms are too, pour the sauce over them. Cover and let them simmer until tender to the fork. It will take about ½ to ¾ of an hour, depending on the thickness of your pork chops, the heat you use, and how many you are cooking, so keep checking them. When they are tender to the fork, remove from the heat. You can use the mushroom sauce as a gravy over the meat or potatoes.

For a change, you can use the sauce recipe as above, except use the can of cream of onion soup with minced onions instead of a can of mushrooms. It is a good variety and gives them a good flavor. You can use sliced onions, too, in with the onion soup.

# Pork Teriyaki

pork tenderloin                     Accent
  (½-lb. per person)                Teriyaki Marinade
pork loin, boneless                 Hickory smoke barbecue sauce
¼ cup vegetable oil                 Liquid Smoke

*This is one of my favorite recipes.*
Cut the tenderloin in pieces and marinate, depending on how strong you want the flavor, 2 to 4 hours, or 12 hours, or 24 hours for a good strong flavor. You can also control the flavor by cooking in the Dutch oven. The longer it cooks in the marinade sauce the stronger it gets. Accent all pieces to taste.
Put oil in the Dutch oven and put in pieces of marinated tenderloin. Brown on all sides. Cover. Keep the heat medium, checking every 15 to 20 minutes. Add the marinade sauce and simmer until tender, about 1 to 1½ hours, depending on the amount you are cooking. Pork Teriyaki makes an excellent main dish. Serve it with rice or potatoes.
My quick marinade recipe I make with two 12-ounce bottles of Teriyaki Marinade, 1 tablespoon Wright's Liquid Smoke, and half of an 8-ounce bottle of Hickory Smoke Barbecue Sauce.

# Meat Loaf

1-lb. lean ground beef              ¼ cup milk
1 egg                               2 Tbsp. dry onions
½ cup dry bread crumbs *or*
  cracker crumbs

Mix all the ingredients together. Form them into a loaf shape, and place it in the center of the oven. Pour one can of either cream of onion, cream of mushroom, or cream of tomato soup over it.
Use your 10" Dutch oven if you have one; a larger one will work, too. Level your oven. Put in the meat loaf. Don't use too much heat on the bottom; just enough to help cook it. Put most of the heat on top. After you put the lid on, it will cook in

about 45 minutes to an hour; but, as in all the cooking, check it to make sure it is okay and looking like it should. Serves 6 to 8 people.

This makes an excellent meat loaf. If there is any left over, it will make good sandwiches the next day.

For a 14" oven, we just triple the above quantities. It took 1 hour and 5 minutes to cook, fed 12 and made 3 sandwiches the next day. This will give you an idea of what size to use. The people who ate it said that it was the best meat loaf they had ever tasted. So, perhaps it's worth a try!

To help stretch your food dollar, substitute ½ of the meat with T.V.P., soy bean, beef flavor. It is high in protein and low in cost. When mixed half-and-half with the meat, you won't even know it is there. Let the T.V.P. soak in warm water for about 10 minutes before you mix it with the meat. Then just follow the directions above.

# Chapter Four

# Meat with Vegetables

## Beef Pot Pie with Biscuits

14" Dutch oven to serve
  10 to 12
4 lbs. good boneless lean
  meat
8 medium potatoes
4 onions

6 carrots
1 celery heart
¼ cup vegetable oil or bacon
  grease
2 cups Bisquick

    While you are waiting for the fire to get ready, cut the meat in bite-size cubes. Salt, pepper, and season to taste. Put the oven down on fire level, add the oil and brown the meat all over. Add 1 cup water. Put lid on to simmer so you can now prepare the vegetables. Cut them in bite-size pieces for the filling.

    After the vegetables are cut up, add them to the meat. Salt and pepper to taste. Cover, continue to cook and check about every 10 to 15 minutes. When about done, spoon on the biscuits for the top. Recover. Add heat to the top. Cook until the biscuits are brown and the vegetables are done. Take off and serve while hot.

    For a quick pot pie, you can use the Mulligan Stew recipe!

    Use all the leftover meat and juice. Cut the raw vegetables in small pieces so that they will cook quickly. Simmer until the vegetables are almost done. Add rest of the leftover cooked vegetables, cut up. Let them simmer until tender and the gravy is thick and not too runny. Spoon on the biscuits for the top. When they are brown, it should be ready (10 to 15 minutes). Keep heat on the top to brown; remember to check it after about 10 minutes to see how it's doing. When brown, remove and serve.

# Biscuit Mix Biscuits

(12" oven size)
Use 2 cups of Bisquick or any quick biscuit mix flour, ½ cup cold water. Mix with a fork to a soft dough. Beat vigorously 20 strokes and then spoon on the top of the meat and vegetables in the Dutch oven. Will make about 10 biscuits.
For a 16" oven, double the recipe.
For a 14" oven, 1½ times should cover it.

# Bob's Game Pot Pie

| | |
|---|---|
| 1 game bird per person (dove, quail, or whatever you have) | 1 head celery ¼ cup vegetable oil 1 potato per person |
| 1 onion | salt and pepper |
| 1 carrot | |

You can use any other vegetables you like or have.

After you level the oven over the heat, add the oil to it. When hot, put in the birds and brown them on all sides, then cover, put heat on the top, and simmer until tender. While the meat is simmering, cut the vegetables up in small pieces, ready to put in oven.

When the birds are done, remove them from the oven to a cutting board and put the vegetables in the oven to start cooking. Add some water if needed.

While vegetables are cooking, take all the meat off the bones, then cut it in bite-size pieces and put these pieces into the oven. Cook until the vegetables are tender. Add biscuits to the whole top of the oven. Remove most of the bottom heat and put it on top to brown the biscuits. (See biscuit recipe above.)

When biscuits are brown, the pot pie should be ready. It will take about 1½ hours to do the pot pie from start to finish.

# Beef Stew

| | |
|---|---|
| ¼ to ½ lb. stew meat per person | 1 medium potato per person ½ medium onion per person |

1 carrot                          ¼ cup vegetable oil
1 small stalk celery              salt, pepper, and Accent

If you want to feed 8, cook 4 lbs. of meat and 8 medium potatoes, 4 onions, 1 small head of celery, and 8 carrots. In a 14" Dutch oven it will serve 8 to 10 well and will take about an hour and a half to cook.

After the fire is ready, pour oil in your Dutch oven. Level it on the fire and brown all the stew meat. Salt, pepper, and Accent to taste, and add 1 cup water to cover the meat. While it is simmering, prepare all the vegetables so that when you have a good broth, they will be ready. I cut the carrots in slices so that they cook faster; then, the potatoes in larger pieces, the onions in quarters, and the celery in slices so it will all be done about the same time.

Let the meat simmer about ½ hour, then take off the lid. When you do, tip it so that the moisture runs back into the oven; then, add all the vegetables, salt and pepper to taste, recover and continue to cook. Check to see how it's doing every 15 minutes or so. After about 30 to 45 minutes, test some of the vegetables and meat with a fork. When done, the fork will go in easily. If done, remove and serve warm.

# Mulligan Stew

any leftover cooked meat          any leftover juice from roast
any leftover vegetables:             or gravy
   potatoes, onions, carrots,
   celery, beans, corn, etc.

When out camping or home, with the price of food what it is, everybody saves all the leftovers and that is where this Mulligan Stew comes in. I think the best one to come out of my Dutch oven was a mixture of steak, pork, and roast and some leftover vegetables and gravy. It was a meal fit for a king! Here is how I made it up:

In your 14" Dutch oven, pour in all the leftover gravy, roast juice, etc. Level your oven on the fire and let it simmer. Add all the leftover meat (from which you should have removed all extra fat and all the bones). While this is simmering, prepare all the new vegetables, raw ones first. Cut these in smaller pieces than for regular beef stew because the meat is already cooked and you want it all done at about the same time. As soon as you have them all cut up, add them to the meat and add more water if you need to. Cook for about 15 to 20 minutes, then add all the leftover vegetables you want to put in—green beans, corn, or whatever you want. Cover up again and cook until the new vegetables are done. You can test them with a fork as before. This is a very tasty meal and helps with the food bill, too!

*Note:* In case you don't have any gravy or juice from the roast left over, and want to whip up a Mulligan Stew, you can use a brown gravy mix package; it will give you a good base for the stew.

## Pot Roast with Vegetables

| | |
|---|---|
| beef roast (½ lb. per person) | 1 medium-size potato per |
| ¼ cup vegetable oil |   person |
| salt and pepper | 6 large carrots |
| ½ onion per person | 1 can whole mushrooms |

Level your Dutch oven over the heat. Pour oil into the oven. When oil is hot, brown roast on all sides. Turn with tongs to keep juices in. Salt and pepper to taste. Cover and cook until meat is medium. Place pared and cut-up vegetables in oven. Turn meat occasionally and watch vegetables so they don't burn. When vegetables are done, the meat should be very tender.

If a gravy is wanted, remove the vegetables and meat and thicken with flour (or as an added taste, add a can of cream of mushroom or cream of onion soup). It really dresses up a roast.

For those of you who enjoy corn on the cob, here is a way to fix it that's simple. Clean corn of husk and silk. Place on top of the roast for the last 15 to 20 minutes of cooking time. This steams the corn and it really goes well with the roast.

## Hunters' Luck Pot Roast with Vegetables

Nothing tastes better after you have been out hunting or fishing all day than to come back to a hot meal. I call this

Hunters' Luck because we fix it when we leave camp and with some luck, it's all ready when we get back.

14" Dutch oven
beef roast (½ lb. per person)
potatoes, carrots, and onions

¼ cup vegetable oil or bacon grease
salt and pepper

Build a regular fire for the coals you will need to cook with. While the fire is burning down, pour the oil in the Dutch oven and prepare the vegetables: quarter the potatoes, slice the carrots in thirds and quarter the onions. Make sure you have a hole dug close by the coals that will be big enough to bury the oven in; about 16" wide by 18" deep should be plenty. When the coals are ready to use, put a good layer in the bottom of the hole. Then put the oven in, level it, and then place the meat and vegetables in the oven. Cover the oven and place coals over it. This will keep it from being stolen while all are away from camp and will give it the heat needed to cook to perfection while you're away. When you return, just uncover the oven and remove it from the coals with your hook, as it will be hot. The meal will be ready and very good.

If you were gone longer than planned, the roast may have a crust on it. If so, just slice it off. The balance of the roast will be good eating.

# Pork Roast with Vegetables

4 lb. pork loin roast (serves 6 to 8)
salt, pepper, Accent
¼ cup vegetable oil

assorted vegetables: new potatoes, carrots, corn-on-the cob

Salt and pepper and Accent all sides of the roast.

After the oil is in the Dutch oven, put on medium to hot coals until the roast is scored on all sides, then cover and simmer. Check it every 20 to 30 minutes. After 1 to 1½ hours, put in vegetables of your choice and let cook with meat until tender and vegetables are done. I have never tasted a vegetable that didn't taste good cooked like this. After drawing off the grease, you can use the juices as a natural gravy for meat and vegetables.

If you cook the corn on a cob, put in the last few minutes with heat on top and bottom. It will take only 15 to 20 minutes or less to cook them.

# Hamburger Steak with Onions or Mushrooms

ground round
  ½-lb. per adult
  ¼-lb. per child
  ¼ to ½ onion per person

1 can cream of onion soup
salt, pepper, and Accent
¼ cup vegetable oil or shortening (bacon grease is best)

While your fire is getting ready for cooking, peel your onions and dice them up finely, then mold in with the ground round to make individual steaks. Salt and pepper and Accent to taste.

On level Dutch oven, pour in oil. When it's hot, put in the steaks and brown on both sides, then cover to let them simmer while you prepare the onion sauce. Open 1 can of cream of onion soup. Put in bowl, add 1 can of milk and stir until smooth. Take the lid off of the oven and turn over steaks. Pour the sauce over them, cover and cook until done. Fifteen minutes should do it. These should be the best burger steaks you have ever eaten.

If you want a change, you can use cream of mushroom soup; it is very good, too.

We ran out of soup once, but had a bunch of onions. I just sliced up the onions and browned them in with the steaks. After they were browned I added the mushrooms and let them simmer until the steaks were done. They were delicious this way, too.

# Cube Steak with Mushroom Sauce

cube steak (1 per person)
1 can mushrooms
1 can cream of mushroom soup

salt, pepper, Accent
¼ cup vegetable oil

First, try to select cube steaks with as little fat and gristle as possible, so they won't be too tough.

Salt and pepper and Accent the cube steaks to taste, while your level Dutch oven is heating up with the vegetable oil already in it.

When it gets warm, put in the cube steaks and brown on both sides. After steaks brown, add the extra can of mushrooms and brown them, too. Cover and let simmer for 20 to 30 minutes, checking to see how they are doing and adding more oil if needed. After 30 minutes, add the mushroom sauce to the steaks. Cover and continue to simmer until tender. This will be about 30 more minutes or so, depending on the heat and how many steaks you are cooking. Potatoes cooked in with the steaks are very good. Just cook them in a separate pan and add when the steaks are about half cooked so they will absorb the flavor of the mushroom sauce.

As a change of flavor, you can use the sauce recipe using the onion sauce. Whichever you use, they will be the best cube steaks you have ever tried.

# Pork Tenderloin w/Mushroom Sauce

pork tenderloin (1 per adult)
¼ cup vegetable oil or
  margarine

1 can cream of mushroom
  soup (per every 4)
salt, pepper, and Accent

*This is also one of my favorite recipes!*
Accent the tenderloin to taste. Cut the tenderloin in pieces, lengthwise, so they are about equal thickness. Pour oil in the Dutch oven. Heat medium to hot and brown on all sides. Cover and let simmer 1 to 1½ hours until almost done, then pour in mushroom sauce and simmer until tender (about 1 hour, more depending on the amount cooking, as in all dishes). Check every 20 minutes or so and turn meat over.

My simple mushroom sauce I make by pouring a can of cream of mushroom soup in a dish and adding a can full of milk to the soup to pour over the tenderloin.

# Liver and Onions

baby beef liver (½-lb. per
  person—2 pieces)

¼ cup vegetable oil (bacon
  grease, if available)

½ medium or large onion      salt, pepper
     per person                  1 cup flour

First, select some good liver to start with. Get baby beef liver if available as it will be more tender than regular beef liver.

Trim the liver into even slices and cut out all the excess gristle and veins. Salt and pepper to taste, then put it in a paper sack with the flour; shake it so you will get a good coating of flour on the liver.

Level your Dutch oven. Put in the ¼ cup bacon grease until it gets hot, then brown the liver on both sides. Cover and let simmer while you cut the onions in slices.

When onions are sliced, add to the liver and bacon grease. Keep turning the liver and onions so they won't stick, but will keep browning. Check every 15 minutes. You can test with a fork; let simmer until tender to the fork.

It should be done in about 45 minutes or so, depending on the amount of heat and how much you are cooking, but it will be *good* when done.

# Chapter Five

# Vegetables

## Quick Dutch Oven Beans

bacon, ½-lb.
1 16-oz. can pork and beans

¼ cup Bar-B-Q Sauce, hickory
 smoked

Cook bacon in oven until crisp...drain off excess grease. Add beans and Bar-B-Cue Sauce. Cover and simmer about 30 minutes. Will serve 12.
For larger groups, add more beans, bacon and sauce. Leave on low heat to keep warm while other foods are cooking.

## Deluxe Dutch Oven Beans

bacon, ½-lb.
1 16-oz. can pork and beans
½ cup of brown sugar
1 Tbsp. vinegar
2 Tbsp. minced onion

½ Tsp. prepared mustard
1 Tsp. molasses
2½ Tbsp. Bar-B-Cue sauce,
 hickory

Cook bacon in oven until crisp, then cut into bite-size pieces. Mix all the ingredients together. Cover and simmer for 30 minutes. Stir at least once to check cooking and to be sure it doesn't cook too fast.
Will serve 8 to 12. If cooking for larger groups, add more beans and bacon. For 20 to 24 people, double it.

## Dutch Oven French Fries

1 large potato per person
½ gallon vegetable oil

14" Dutch oven
salt to taste

When camping out, everybody enjoys a steak barbeque, which is fine. I like steak too, and with it I enjoy good, fresh, French fries. Try this recipe with your next cookout.

These are the best French fries I have ever eaten.... Try them; you will like them too.

Place oven on heat, add oil, make sure it is level.

Cut the potatoes, in even small-sized pieces. Add to oil which should be hot. Let them simmer. Be sure you use enough oil.... The fries should be covered. Done when golden brown and floating in oil. They will take about 20 to 30 minutes, depending upon how many you are fixing...and the temperature of the heat.

The oil can be reused again. Strain, if necessary and return to the bottle for next time.

When fries are done, drain excess oil on paper towels. Add salt and pepper to taste. Best fries you ever tasted.

# Potatoes and Onions

1 large potato per person          ¼ cup vegetable oil or short-
½ onion per person                    ening (bacon grease is best)
salt and pepper

This is one of the most popular side dishes cooked in Dutch ovens.

Slice potatoes in even slices. I use a small square vegetable grater with a slicer on one side; it is quick and does a good job. Cut onions in quarters as they will break up. They don't have to be sliced.

Pour oil in the oven and put it on heat. Put on potatoes and onions, salt and pepper to taste, then cover and apply heat to top also so they can brown on the top and bottom at the same time.

Check them every 10 to 15 minutes. Turn with a spatula to rotate them. Add more oil if needed, a little at a time, so as not to get too oily. Cook until tender to fork.

Cooking time will depend on how many potatoes you are cooking and how much heat you use. A 14" Dutch oven full will take about an hour to cook.

I can cook 20 pounds in my 16" oven in about 1 hour (16 pounds of potatoes, 4 pounds of onions) which will feed 25 to 30 people, depending on how much they like potatoes.

If you have to cook more than that, use several Dutch ovens. A 16" oven will serve about 25 to 30 and a 14" oven about 15 to 20, unless you eat a lot of potatoes. But, remember, they cook way down. You start with a full oven; when they are done they will cook down about ½, so allow for cooking down and the size of servings.

# Deluxe Potatoes and Onions

If you have some bacon and the time, it adds extra flavor to the potatoes and onions to add about ½ to 1 pound cooked bacon to them. Just start off with the bacon in the level Dutch oven. Cut it up into pieces. Cook until crisp. Add potatoes and onions to the grease and cook as before except the bacon will give extra flavor. Don't wait until it is too crisp to start it as it may get too done by the time the potatoes and onions are done.

# Chapter Six

# Dutch Oven Quick Meals

## Link Sausage and Beans

pork link sausages (4 to 6 per
  person)
salt and pepper

1 can oven baked beans (16 oz.
  can will serve about 6 to 8)

This is one of my favorite quick Dutch oven meals. We fix it a lot out camping when fishing or hunting because it is easy, quick, and good eating.

The size oven you use will depend on how much you want to cook. If you only want to fix enough for 6 to 8, use 1 can of beans. A 10" oven will be big enough and 24 to 30 link sausages can feed them all. For more you can add more beans and sausages and go to a 12" or 14" oven.

When the fire is ready, brown your sausages on all sides. Drain off the excess grease, then pour in the beans. If too thick, add a little water or barbecue sauce, just so they will stir. Salt and pepper to taste. Put cover on and simmer for 15 to 20 minutes. They will be worth the effort. You will have found a good use for link sausages besides breakfast.

## Dutch Oven Bar-B-Que Hot Dogs

1 package weiners
10" Dutch oven

1 large bottle hickory smoke
  barbecue sauce

Put the oven on; keep the heat just high enough to simmer slowly, so the flavor of the sauce will soak into the weiners. Pour in the sauce, then, while it is heating, carefully score each weiner along the side so it will get the flavor of the sauce. Cover and let simmer about 20 to 30 minutes. You can serve it in regular hot dog buns or slice and put on bread as a sandwich.

As an added treat, if you like cheese, try some shredded cheese on top of the hot weiner. You can use the sauce as you would catsup. It is good! Make sure you save what is left over for next time, for you can use it on ribs or chicken. We save it by putting it back in a screw-top bottle and refrigerating it until we need it again.

# Bar-B-Que Beef Sandwiches

1 roast (¼-lb. meat per sandwich, in figuring size of
roast to cook)
large bottle hickory flavor barbecue sauce

salt, pepper, and Accent
¼ cup vegetable oil or
margarine
chopped onion

Use 10 to 12" Dutch oven, depending on how much you fix. Because you will be using this for sandwiches, an economy cut of meat will be fine. They have a good flavor and with a little extra cooking time will come out fine when they are cut up. No one will care, they will be so good!

Make your oven level. Pour in oil. Brown roast on all sides, then salt and pepper and Accent to taste. Cover, add heat to the top and let simmer, checking every 15 minutes or so. Depending on the size and shape of the roast, in about an hour it should be ready for you to take the meat off the bone (if any). I like to pull mine apart in strips, removing all excess fat and bone. While doing this, let the juice from the roast simmer slowly. Using a spoon, dip out any extra grease, then pour in the barbecue sauce to thicken the juice that was in the oven. It may take the whole bottle.

You can now add the meat you have prepared to the flavorful mixture of roast juice and hickory barbecue sauce. Simmer for about 30 minutes to let the meat absorb the flavor. I think it makes the best barbecue sandwiches. I hope you agree.

As a change, you can use the same recipe for hamburger— for Sloppy Joes.

Cook the hamburger in a small amount of bacon grease until done. Break up the hamburger and add the barbecue sauce. Let simmer in the sauce for at least 15 minutes to flavor the meat, and it will be ready to dish out for "Sloppy Joe Burgers"!

# Dutch Oven Weiners and Beans

1 package weiners
½ lb. bacon
1 can pork and beans (16 oz.)
  or oven baked beans
½ cup brown sugar

1 Tbsp. vinegar
2 Tbsp. minced onion
½ Tsp. prepared mustard
½ Tsp. molasses
2 Tbsp. barbecue sauce

Cook the bacon until crisp, then cut it in bite-size pieces. Drain off the excess grease and put back on heat. Add all the other ingredients except the weiners (they will be put in later). Stir and let simmer while you are cutting the weiners in pieces. I cut each one into about 4 pieces, so the cut ends will absorb the good flavor of the beans and sauce while they heat up, but you can cut them up in any size you like or leave them whole if you want.

When you have these cut the way you want them, put them in with the simmering beans. Stir them up, cover and let simmer about 20 to 30 minutes. They will be ready then. Check at least once between times to make sure it is not cooking too hot or too slowly.

This will be a main dish and one even the kids should enjoy. For an added treat, sprinkle with shredded cheese; it will add extra flavor.

# Chapter Seven

# Poultry and Fish

## Dutch Oven Chicken

chicken          salt, pepper
(½ per adult, ¼ per child,   flour
or 2-3 pieces per adult,    ½ cup vegetable oil
1-2 per child)           or shortening

While Dutch oven is heating up with the oil in it, put the flour in a sack, put the chicken pieces in it, and shake to cover them with flour. Salt and pepper to taste. Put in oven and brown on all sides. Cover and simmer until tender. Put heat on top as well as bottom to cook faster.

If you like a certain piece of chicken, it is best to buy them only, as they are all the same size and they will be done in a more unified time.

Another tip: if cooking for a large group, use some ovens for browning with more oil in, and after browning well put them in other ovens to steam with only a little oil. Check them to rotate chicken so that bottom and top pieces don't get too well done.

For another variation, you can also use a good barbecue sauce while they are steaming. Add about a quart of sauce, for a 14" oven. It will give it a good flavor.

You can make your own or use any good sauce ready made.

With either regular or barbecue, check every 10 to 15 minutes to see how it's doing, until tender to the fork, then serve.

If you are cooking for a large group, some chicken will always be done first, but that doesn't have to be a problem.

Cut way down on the heat and just let it stay warm and it will be fine.

# Dutch Oven Roast Turkey Ala/Bob

½ small turkey, 6 to 8 lbs.          ¼ cup vegetable oil
salt and pepper                      or bacon grease
14" or 16" oven

I always wanted to cook a turkey in a Dutch oven, but because they are too big for the oven, I had to settle for a half of a turkey. The butcher will be happy to cut a turkey in half for you. After you have tried it, you will be glad for the other half to try again. Everyone that has eaten it says that a Dutch oven cooked turkey is the best.
    Here is how to do it:
    *Let the turkey defrost before you cook it.*
    Level the oven on the heat and add the oil. When hot, put the turkey in and salt and pepper to taste. Then brown it on all sides until good and brown.
    Add 1 cup water, put the lid on the oven, add coals to the top and let it simmer. Check it about every 20 minutes—stir up the juice and turn the turkey over each time so both sides will have the flavor and not be dry as most oven-cooked turkeys are. Also add water if needed. It will take about 2½ hours to cook an 8-lb. turkey, 3 hours for 10 to 12 lbs., but it will be the best turkey you ever tasted.
    Test it by sticking with fork when done. Serve while warm and use the juice in the oven as a special treat, pouring it over the meat and the potatoes or rice.
    I hope you will agree this is a special treat and the best turkey you ever had too. If there is any left over, use it for sandwiches the next day. Because it has more flavor and is not dry, it makes very special sandwiches, too.

# Trout Ala/Bob

trout, fresh, 1 to 2 per person      flour
¼ cup bacon grease                   salt and pepper

This is a recipe that will come in handy if you want to feed people fresh trout when you are out camping. They are very tasty and quick to prepare. Try a side dish of potatoes and onions in bacon grease with them.

First, wash the trout in clean, cold water and remove their heads. This is optional, to provide for more room in the oven. Then, flour on both sides and salt and pepper to taste (use paper sack for flour; it is quicker if you have one). Heat and level the Dutch oven. Put in bacon grease; when hot, put in the trout. Cook about 10 minutes until golden brown, then turn over and cook until golden brown (10 minutes) on the other side, too. After browning, you can put them in a separate Dutch oven to cook slowly and keep warm while additional trout are being cooked to the same golden brown.

As you cook them with the bones in, I can tell you how I remove the bones for easy eating and it works well. I like to cook them when they are fresh and this makes them curl up a little bit, but the flavor is much better and the bones come out the same.

Remove all the fins and cut off the tail. Then hold the cooked fish by the large center bone with one hand. Using a fork in the other hand, peel the meat off the bone down to the end, then turn it over and repeat on the other side. If you don't like to eat the skin, you can turn the halves over and peel the skin off. To make sure you have all the bones out, rake along the meat with the fork and it will show if any are left. Remove any bones you find. Add a little lemon juice, a dash of salt and pepper and sit down and enjoy the feast.

If you plan to cook potatoes and onions with the trout, put them on first. It will take them 30 to 45 minutes to cook, depending on how many you cook, and the fish will cook in 20 to 25 minutes.

A 14" Dutch oven will brown six to eight 12" pan-size fish at a time. A 16" Dutch oven will brown ten to twelve 12" pan-size fish at a time.

# Chapter Eight

# Desserts

## Tips on Cooking Dutch Oven Desserts

Before you get into the desserts, I would like to give a few tips on what desserts you can cook in a Dutch oven and how to do it. *Cobblers, quick cake, pies, cookies, pineapple upside-down cake* are some of the desserts I have fixed out camping, and they surely perk up a meal. So with that in mind, we will cover all the above one at a time.

### *Cobblers*

Cobblers are one of the most popular desserts, so it comes first, with tips on what to do and what not to do. When camping out, it is easier to use cake mixes and canned pie filling or canned fruit for the cobblers. *Do not* put the eggs in the cake mix, as they make it raise too high and stick to the oven.

When using fresh fruit, you can make up a simple syrup if the fruit needs moisture. If using bottled fruit, keep the size small. If necessary, slice the pieces smaller. Also, don't use all of the juice, use only enough to cover up the fruit. If you want to thicken the juice that comes in the canned berries, use two large tablespoons of cornstarch for each four cans of fruit and mix it up with the fruit in a separate bowl. Then pour it in the oven and pour the cake mix over it as evenly as possible. It will sink into the fruit, but when it starts cooking, it will raise up again and bake.

When mixing up the cake mix, use a separate bowl for each cobbler. Do not use the eggs as explained above, but add ¼ cup extra water. Mix it until smooth and still thin enough to pour. I use the yellow or the white cake mix the most often.

You can also use the golden pound cake or your own recipe from scratch if you have all the items you need with you. Remember, when using the golden pound cake, it doesn't go as far as the regular cake mix, but it has a good flavor. For how much to use, see the chart at the end of this Tip Section.

When you bake cobblers or any other dessert, it does not take much heat on the bottom of the oven. If the oven is lined with aluminum foil, use about 4 to 6 briquets, or 1 shovel of coals on the bottom and most of the heat on top, about 18 to 24 briquets or 3 shovels of coals.

When using aluminum foil to line the oven, try to use one piece without a seam—it will help keep juice out and be easier to clean. You can roll down the edge inside of the oven, or cut it off with a knife, level with the top edge of the oven. This is to make sure the aluminum foil doesn't keep the oven lid from making a good seal.

A cobbler should cook in about 30 to 40 minutes in a 14" oven, 20 to 30 minutes in a 12" oven. If you have a 16" oven, it will take 45 to 50 minutes to cook. I still check all my cobblers after 15 minutes to make sure everything is okay. I have made hundreds of them over the years and never lost one so far. It is always a good idea to check on whatever you are cooking to avoid something going wrong, like having too much heat, or not enough heat, on the top or bottom.

Knowing the right amount of heat will come with practice. When the top of the cobbler you are checking is a golden brown and cracking slightly, it should be done. To test it, put a knife into the cake. If it is cooked, the cake ingredients will not stick to the knife. If it is not done inside but is a golden brown on the outside, remove some of the heat on top, then check every 5 minutes until it is done. Cooking time will be different in higher elevations and depending on the heat used, so learn to check often.

After you learn these basic tips and methods, you will want to try a new fruit or a combination of fruit cobblers for yourself. Don't be afraid to try one out. Who knows, you may have a real winner and the practice will be good for you.

When your cobbler is done, let it cool for a couple of minutes while you get the ice cream ready. Serve it warm, with ice cream or Cool Whip or whatever you have.

These cobblers are worth the work involved. I hope you agree after trying some of them. We all have our favorite.

Mine is red or black raspberry. Try them all and see what
yours will be.

## QUICK GUIDE FOR COBBLERS:

| | | |
|---|---|---|
| 16" oven | 7 to 8 cans of filling | 2 cake mixes or 3 golden pound cakes |
| 14" oven | 4 cans of filling | 1 cake mix or 2 golden pound cakes |
| 12" oven | 3 cans of filling | 1 cake mix or 1½ golden pound cakes |
| 10" oven | 2 cans of filling | ½ cake mix or 1 golden pound cake |

You can add more cans of filling and more cake too. It
will go further, but you must allow more cooking time. I have
used up to 10 cans in a 16" oven and 6 cans in a 14" oven.
Regular cobblers serve 25 people in a 16", 15 with a 14", and
about 10 with a 12" and 6 with a 10". You can serve about 30
people in a 16" oven with the two extra cans and 20 with a 14"
oven with the two extra cans of filling.

### Quick Cake

There are several different brands and kinds on the market—just pick out the one you like best, mix it up as per the
instructions, pour it in a cake pan, and put the pan and all in
the oven. Bake the same amount of time as it says. Then
check to see if it is done. It usually will take a little longer to
cook than it would in your regular oven at home. A Dutch oven-
cooked cake sure is good for a snack with a glass of cold milk.

### Baking Pies and Cookies

It is easy to bake a pie when you're out camping, just mix
up your favorite recipe, then put it in the pie tin as if you were
home. Put the pie tin in the oven on 3 rocks or pieces of rolled
up aluminum foil to keep the pie level and off the bottom. The
rocks or aluminum foil work as a shelf would in your oven.
They let the heat circulate around the pie. You can do this

same thing when you bake cookies—just be sure your cookie sheet will fit inside the oven.

A good warm apple pie or batch of cookies can give you a real pick-up after a hard day fishing or hunting or just enjoying the great outdoors.

Here is a pie crust recipe I use of my wife's that makes good pie crust almost foolproof. A good pie will always add that extra-special finishing touch to a meal.

# #1 Super Pie Crust

2½ cups of flour          1 Tsp. of salt
1 cup of shortening (be   1 pinch of baking powder
generous)

Mix well.

Break 1 egg (save some of the white to put on the top of your crust)
Add 1 Tbsp. of vinegar
¼ cup of water

Mix all ingredients together with your hands. Don't be afraid to really mix it because it won't hurt it.

This makes enough for two pies (four 9" crusts).

When the crust is ready, use one can of apple pie filling in the bottom crust, add a sprinkle of cinnamon, and then put on the top crust. Put it in a level 14" oven on the rack, or three pieces of rolled up aluminum foil. Put the cover on the oven and put about 8 to 10 briquets on the bottom and 18 to 20 on top. Cook until golden brown, about 30 to 45 minutes. Test to make sure it's done, then serve warm with ice cream or cheese and cold milk.

You can cook whatever kind of pie you like this way: cherry, strawberry, etc.

### Pineapple Upside Down Cake

The recipe is included in this book and it tells you how to make one, but here are a couple of good tips to remember. When you roll the aluminum foil inside the oven, do it so you can lift it out when done and can tip it over on a cutting board so the glazing is on top.

Test it like the cobblers. When done, serve it warm, with Cool Whip or ice cream.

### Cookies

The first step with chocolate chip cookies is mixing up a batch to cook. Just follow the recipe on the package of chips. If you are in a hurry, the readymade frozen ones are good, as are the rolled cookies you just have to cut in pieces. All of these work well. Just keep them in a cooler until you want to cook them, then take them out, cut them up and put on a pizza pan or cookie sheet and you are ready.

Next step is to get the oven on the coals or briquets as level as you can. Put rocks in the oven, or rolled up aluminum foil, to make a shelf for the cookie sheet. Put the cookie sheet (12") or pizza pan in the oven (14"). Put the lid on, and add the coals to the top. Use about 18 briquets on top and 12 on the bottom. The cookies will cook in almost the same time as they would in your home oven: 12 to 15 minutes. When brown, take off the lid and remove the cookies to a cooling board with a spatula. Then you can put more cookies on the pan to cook.

A 12" cookie sheet inside a 14" oven will hold about 18 cookies if you don't make them too big. They will go over so well you will have to cook several batches for all to enjoy.

Try the same procedure for sugar cookies or whatever your favorite cookie is.

# Apple Cobbler

14" Dutch oven
4 cans apple pie filling
2 to 3 Tsp. cinnamon

1 package yellow cake mix, *or*
2 packages golden pound
cake

Before preparing the oven for use, line it with aluminum foil. This makes it easier to clean. Be sure not to place the foil too close to the top, thus hindering lid from closing.

In a separate bowl mix the 4 cans of apple pie filling. Do not use canned applesauce—it is too mushy and does not make good cobbler.

In a second bowl, mix up your cake mix until smooth; don't add the eggs, rather add an extra ¼ cup water. The batter should be thick, yet thin enough to pour.

Level your oven. Pour in your apple mixture and smooth it out. Sprinkle on the cinnamon, then pour the cake mixture on top. Cover. Put heat on top and bottom. It should cook in 25 to 30 minutes. Check at 15 minutes. A final check can be made when the cake is golden brown and cracking.

Serve with ice cream for a real treat—it's a dish fit for anyone.

If you prefer to use a golden pound cake on this cobbler, use 2 packages. Mix as you would the cake mix. Allow about 5 to 10 minutes more for cooking time. Also, the cake will be a little thicker.

# Cherry Cobbler

14" Dutch oven                    1 yellow cake mix, *or* 2 pkgs.
4 cans cherry pie filling         golden pound cake

While waiting for the fire to get hot, line the oven with aluminum foil. Make sure it doesn't interfere with the closing of the lid.

In a separate bowl mix the cake mix until smooth, or the pound cakes if you prefer them,....the batter should be thick yet still thin enough to pour. Add the 4 cans of cherry pie filling into the Dutch oven. Place on the fire. Be sure the oven is level. Pour the cake mix on top. Add the lid and check the bottom heat. The cobbler should cook in 30 to 35 minutes. Allow 30 to 40 minutes when using pound cake. Still check every 15 minutes to control cooking. As with other cobblers, check it with a fork or knife for doneness when it is golden brown and cracking. Remove from oven and serve with ice cream.

Because cherry is not one of my favorite cobblers, I have never made one using fresh cherries. However, you cherry lovers could try one by using 2 cups, 8 oz. each, of fresh cherries for each can of pie filling, then adding 1 cup of simple syrup for sweetness. Cover with the cake mix and cook as above. Those big, Bing cherries and special pie cherries might make an excellent cobbler. Try it and you could be in for a pleasant surprise.

# Blackberry Cobbler

14" Dutch oven
4 cans of blackberries

2 rounded Tbsp. of cornstarch
1 yellow cake mix

While waiting for the fire to get hot, line the oven with aluminum foil. Make sure it doesn't interfere with the closing of the lid. The lid must fit tightly.

In a separate bowl mix the 4 cans of blackberries with the 2 rounded tablespoons of cornstarch for thickening. They must be well mixed.

In the second bowl, mix the cake batter. Remember, no eggs. Add about ¼ cup extra water to make the mixture smooth, yet thin enough to pour.

Level the oven before adding the blackberries. Smooth out and pour the cake batter on top. Cover. Add heat to the top. Check the bottom heat. Cooking time is 30 to 35 minutes. Make 15 minute checks also.

Remove from heat. Serve with ice cream while warm. You will see why my preference is this cobbler and the red raspberry.

# Red Raspberry Cobbler

14" Dutch oven
4 cans red raspberries
1 yellow cake mix

2 rounded Tbsp. cornstarch
roll of large aluminum foil

An option to you—lining the oven with aluminum foil for easier clean-up after cooking. It is timesaving when cooking for a large group when clean-up time follows. Line the oven as mentioned on previous pages...allow for tight cover closure.

Mix fruit and cornstarch in one bowl. In another bowl, prepare the cake mix. Remember, use no eggs, but add ¼ cup water instead.

The Dutch oven will be heating and when ready, add the fruit mixture. Follow by adding the cake mixture (excess juice over fruit should be spooned off if necessary).

When using foil, use 8 to 10 briquets on bottom or one shovel of coals. Cooking time is 30 to 35 minutes. Test the heat and watch that it doesn't get too brown. Adjust heat by removing some coals, if necessary.

Remove when done. Let it cool about 5 minutes. Serve with ice cream. This is my favorite of all the cobblers.

# Peach Cobbler

14" Dutch oven                    4 16-oz. cans sliced peaches,
1 yellow cake mix                 or 3 quarts bottled peaches,
                                  sliced

Line the Dutch oven with aluminum foil. Do not let the foil interfere with the closing of the cover. It must fit tightly so no heat will escape.

Place the canned peaches in the Dutch oven. Be sure it is level. Add the cake mixture (leave out the eggs—use ¼ cup water instead). The mixture should be thick, yet thin enough to pour. The cake will cook in 30 to 35 minutes. Check periodically, each 15 minutes or so.

When using bottled peaches, most of which are in halves, place them in a bowl so they can be sliced. These may need to be thickened; if so, add 1 Tbsp. cornstarch for each bottle of fruit. Add them to the Dutch oven with about half of the juice. Add more juice if it needs it—the peaches should just be covered.

The cake mix should be prepared and then added on top. Cover with the lid, adding heat to the top. It will cook in 25 to 30 minutes. Make 15 minute checks.

Should the juice bubble up through the cake, take it off with a big spoon. Let it cook some more. When brown on top, test it as the others with a fork or knife.

Serve with ice cream while still warm.

# Pineapple Cobbler

14" Dutch oven                    1 yellow cake mix
4 cans crushed pineapple

Line your Dutch oven with aluminum foil, as with previous cobblers, allowing room for the cover to fit tightly.

In a separate bowl, mix the cake batter. Use no eggs, use ¼ cup water instead. The mixture should be thick but yet should pour.

Level the Dutch oven, then add the crushed pineapple. Smooth it out, and then add the cake mixture on top. Cover and apply heat to the top. Cooking time should be 30 to 35 minutes. Make 15 minute checks.

If the juice should boil through the cake mix, remove the excess with a big spoon. Return to the heat and cook some more. Some brands of pineapple are more juicy than others. The excess juice should be removed. The fruit need only be covered before adding the cake mixture.

When golden brown and cracking, test the cake with a knife or fork. When done, remove it from the heat and cool it for a few minutes. This is one cobbler on which I prefer to use whipped cream instead of ice cream. It is an excellent treat either way. When using whipped cream, allow the cobbler to cool more to avoid the melting of the cream.

# Strawberry Cobbler

14" Dutch oven                         1 yellow cake mix
4 cans strawberries                    3 rounded Tbsp. cornstarch

Canned strawberries are an excellent substitute for fresh strawberries when fresh ones are not available. Frozen berries may also be used. (See fresh cobbler for amount.)

Berries and cornstarch are mixed in one bowl; the cake mix, less the eggs, in the second bowl. Extra water may be added if too thick. The batter must be pourable.

Level the Dutch oven, add the fruit mixture, then cover with the cake mixture. Cover, and cooking should be completed within 30 to 35 minutes. Make 15 minute checks. When brown and cracking, check the cake for doneness with a fork or knife. Serve warm with ice cream. If using whipped cream, the cake should be slightly cooled.

# Fresh Red Raspberry Cobbler

14" Dutch oven                         7 10-oz. packages of frozen
3 rounded Tbsp. cornstarch            raspberries

1 yellow cake mix                 9 cups fresh, red raspberries
1 cup simple syrup (2 parts       (8-oz. cups)
   sugar—1 part water)

This is my favorite cobbler. One cannot always find canned red raspberries, but the frozen or fresh are as good as canned, or better. You can be the judge.

Mix the fruit and simple syrup in a separate bowl. The cake mix is prepared in a second bowl.

After lining the Dutch oven with foil, be sure it is level, then add the prepared fruit followed by the cake mix. Cover and add to heat. Follow up by checking in 15 minutes.

*Using frozen fruit:* Let packages thaw before adding thickening. It will be easier to mix. Follow through as above. The cake should cook in 30 to 35 minutes. When golden brown and cracking, test for doneness with a fork or knife. Let cool for a few minutes, then serve with ice cream. It will be an excellent treat.

# Fresh Peach Cobbler

8 cups fresh peaches          1 yellow cake mix, *or*
1 cup simple syrup (2 parts   2 golden pound cake mixes
   sugar; 1 part water) *or*
   1 cup pineapple juice, if you
   prefer

Line the Dutch oven with aluminum foil, if you wish. Do not let the foil hinder the lid from closing completely.

In separate bowls, slice the peaches, then add the simple syrup or pineapple juice, whichever you prefer. I have used both, but lean towards the pineapple juice for extra flavor. I think you should try them both and see which you like best.

In the other bowl, mix up the cake mix, with no eggs, adding the extra water until smooth. It should still be able to pour.

Level the oven. Pour in the fruit and syrup mixture. Add the cake batter. Cover and add heat to top of oven. Remember, fresh fruit cobblers will take more time and heat to cook. Heat is also applied to the bottom. Follow up with 15 minute checks. The cobbler should cook within 30 to 40 minutes.

Test with fork or knife when the cake is golden brown and cracking. When finished, serve with ice cream while still warm
You can use this same method with apricots.

# Fresh Strawberry Cobbler

14" Dutch oven
8 cups fresh strawberries
(measuring cups, not fruit
cups), *or* 7 10-oz. packages
of frozen strawberries

1 cup simple syrup, 8-ozs. (2
parts sugar—1 part water)
*or* 1 cup pineapple juice
1 yellow cake mix

Line the oven with aluminum foil, if you like. Place the strawberries in one bowl (cutting large ones if necessary, add the syrup, mix with berries. I have used both fruit juice and pineapple juice, and both work very well. Which you use is your choice.

The cake mixture is prepared in a second bowl. Use no eggs, ¼ cup of extra water should be added to keep mixture pourable.

Level the Dutch oven. Add fruit, level it off, then add the cake mix on top. Add cover. Fresh cobblers take more heat and a little longer time to cook. Leave more heat on the bottom, still making 15 minute checks. It should be done in 30 to 40 minutes.

When golden brown and cracking, test it as before with a knife or a fork. Remove from heat and let cool about 5 minutes. Serve warm with ice cream or, when cool, whipped cream makes a nice change.

# Dutch Oven Quick Cake

10" Dutch oven — 1 package
Snack 'N' Cake (8 to 10
servings)
Pam vegetable spray

14" Dutch oven — 2 packages
Snack 'N' Cake (14 to 16
servings)

This is a quick and easy treat that is very tasty.

Spray the oven with Pam vegetable spray, unless using a cake pan.

Prepare the cake mixtures in a separate bowl. Be sure the Dutch oven is level. Pour in the cake mixtures and level. Use only a small amount of heat on the bottom. Add the lid and add heat to it.

It will take only about 20 minutes to cook the cake, so it will need close watching. When brown on top and cracking, it can be tested by a knife or a fork. It can be cut while in the oven and served warm with ice cream. This is a special treat to be used when camping. Chocolate chip is my favorite, but there are six varieties to choose from. Try them all and pick out the one you prefer.

If you prefer, you can use a small cake pan. Put the cake mix in the pan and put the pan and all in the oven to cook. It is easy to cook it this way and the clean-up time is almost eliminated.

# Pineapple Upside Down Cake

1 can pineapple (6 slices)          2 yellow cake mixes, *or*
½ cup pecans                        3 golden pound cakes
½ cup brown sugar                   1 14" Dutch oven
1 square butter

Line the oven with aluminum foil, place oven on the heat, level it, and melt the butter in the oven. When melted, add the brown sugar, then the pineapple slices, then the pecans. This will be the glaze.

In a separate bowl, you should have the cake all mixed and ready while the butter is melting in the oven.

This dessert doesn't require much heat on the bottom, just enough to brown the glaze—about 8 briquets should be plenty. As with all baking, most of the heat should be on top. As this cake has no filling, it will cook faster than the cobblers do, in about 25 minutes. Also, remember, because there is no filling, it will only serve 10 to 12 people, so you may have to cook two or more for a group.

Check it every 15 minutes and when golden brown, test it to see if it is done. If it is, take off the heat and lift the cake out of the oven by the aluminum foil. Put a pan or board on it and then turn it over quickly so that the glaze is on top. Remove the foil and you have a special treat. Serve with Cool Whip or ice cream.

# Chapter Nine

# Breads and Rolls

## Baking Breads

Most everyone has their favorite bread recipe. Just use the one you like best and I am sure it will work fine. I have cooked several different kinds and they are all good.

Just mix up your batch of dough to make what you will need. We use eight small tin pans that are 6" long, 3½" wide, and 2" deep. You will have to judge how big a batch to make up. The oven sizes are listed below with the number of these size pans they will hold.

10" oven — 2 pans
12" oven — 3 pans
14" oven — 4 pans
16" oven — 6 pans

A standard batch of dough for two regular sized loaves will make more than enough for four of the small ones. (The eight pans we have were purchased in a local store and can be used for baking banana nut bread, zucchini bread, etc. in your Dutch oven.)

After mixing up your dough as you always do, divide it into the amount of loaves you're going to need. Grease the pans as you do with the regular size, and put the dough in. Let it raise until it reaches the top of the pan. Put in a level Dutch oven, put the lid on, and add the heat (18 to 20 briquets on top and 6 to 8 briquets on the bottom of a 14" oven). Cook until golden brown, about 30 to 40 minutes. Keep your eye on it. It doesn't hurt to check and make sure all is well. When brown on top, take off the heat. Try to serve it while it is still warm.

If you are one of the growing number of people that like sourdough bread, biscuits, or cinnamon rolls, and you have a sourdough starter, try that in a Dutch oven, out camping.

I still remember some of those cinnamon rolls we had for breakfast on several deer hunting trips years ago. These were so good they would almost melt in your mouth. Or how about breaking off a chunk of sourdough bread fresh from the Dutch oven to complement your meal? What a special treat that can be!

Just cook sourdough bread the same as other bread or rolls. With this bread we sometimes have just put in a whole loaf and cooked it all at once. A 10" or 12" ovenfull of bread is surely good and will feed 6 to 8 hungry people, more if not as hungry as we always seem to be.

In case you don't have a sourdough recipe, try this one.

First — Sourdough is a dough that gets its ability to rise from wild yeast spores which flourish in the air. Most other breads use cultured yeast. Once the basic wild yeast, sourdough, has been developed, you can borrow from it when needed. You must replenish your basic starter by paying back what was used. In this way you can keep your own starter for as long as you want it. Keep it in the refrigerator in a glass jar, not in a metal container. Do not mix it with a metal spoon as that will separate the liquids from the batter. Just remove it from the refrigerator and let it stand at room temperature for 30 minutes to 1 hour before use.

# Sourdough Starter

2 cups unsifted all-purpose      1 package active dry yeast
   flour                          1 sourdough packet
2 cups warm water, 90°

Combine all ingredients in large glass or pottery bowl. Mix well with a wooden spoon or rubber scraper. It will be lumpy, but it should be. Cover loosely with wax paper or plastic wrap and let stand in a warm place for 48 hours. The mixture should be bubbly and have a sour aroma (hence the name sourdough). This makes about 2¾ cups of sourdough starter.

This is the mixture you will use on all of the recipes. You must replace what you take from it or you will run out of starter. To replenish the starter add the following to what you have left:

> 2 cups unsifted all-purpose flour
> 2 cups war water, 90°
> 1 Tsp. sugar

Mix well in the large bowl with a wooden spoon. Let it stand in a warm place for 24 hours or until bubbly and sour.

# Sourdough Cinnamon Rolls

Remove two cups of your sourdough starter from the cooler one hour before you prepare this recipe, and make sure you replenish the starter as I told you before in the Sourdough Section.

6 cups unsifted all-purpose
  flour
1 package active dry yeast
½ cup sugar
2 Tsp. salt
⅓ cup softened butter or
  margarine

1 cup hot water
2 cups sourdough starter
melted butter for brushing on
  on dough

Combine 1 cup flour, yeast, sugar, and salt in a large bowl. Mix well with a wooden spoon. Add butter and hot water. Beat for several minutes, scraping down the sides to mix it well. Add the sourdough starter and 1 cup of flour. Beat vigorously for two minutes.

Gradually stir in enough of the remaining flour with the wooden spoon to make a soft dough that leaves the side of the bowl. Put it on a floured board and knead it 8 to 10 minutes, or until the dough is smooth and springy.

Divide the dough in half. Roll each half into a rectangle (about 15" long). Brush each lightly with the melted butter, then sprinkle each rectangular piece of dough with 1 cup of the cinnamon filling (recipe for filling follows). Make sure to cover all the dough. Press the filling lightly into the dough, then roll up each piece of dough jelly roll fashion and seal edges. Cut the rolled dough in 1" slices. Place the cut side up in a greased pan. Cover them with plastic wrap and a towel. Let them rise in a warm place until double in size—about 1½ hours.

This will make 30 rolls, so you can judge how many you will need for all to try. If you need more just double the recipe.

For cooking them you can use several ovens and cook them all at once, or use one 14" oven and cook one batch at a time. A 14" oven will handle about 12 at a time, depending on how big they have risen when you start to cook them.

Grease your 14" oven with butter and fill it with the rolls, placed cut-side down. As in all baking, don't use too much heat on the bottom of oven, try about 6 briquets or 1 shovel of coals, and then put 18 to 20 on top of the oven. Cook until golden brown. It will take about 30 to 35 minutes. Be sure to keep an eye on them.

# Cinnamon Filling

⅓ cup melted butter or
  margarine
1 cup light brown sugar
1 Tsp. cinnamon

1/8 Tsp. cloves
1 cup finely chopped nuts
  (walnuts or pecans)

Mix all the ingredients together until well mixed up. Makes two cups—one for each rectangle of the dough.

As you can see by the time and work required, this is not a quick, effortless dessert. But it can surely perk up a long day, and put the final touch to a meal. So for a special time, try this extra special treat.

# Rolls

Rolls can be baked in a Dutch oven too. They will add an extra special touch to a meal. You may have your own recipe for these breads. If so, try them baked in a Dutch oven when you're out camping and be ready to enjoy a special treat.

For a quick bread, use the bread already in a frozen package. Two loaves in a 10" oven will make an ordinary meal special. There are several breads on the market called Brown and Serve loaves, usually two per package. Brown and serve rolls also add a good touch to a meal.

With the loaves or rolls, just put a lining of aluminum foil in the oven and bake until brown.

In case you don't have a recipe for rolls, try this one.

# Quick Rolls (Serves 12)

| | |
|---|---|
| 1 cup warm water | 1 Tsp. salt |
| 1 package dry yeast | 1 egg |
| 2 Tbsp. sugar | 2 Tbsp. shortening or vege- |
| 2½ cups flour | table oil |

Dissolve yeast in water with sugar. Stir in half the flour. Add the salt. Beat with a spoon until smooth. Add the egg and shortening. Beat in the rest of the flour until smooth.

Cover and let the dough rise until double in size, about 30 minutes. Stir down dough and spoon it into greased oven and let rise until double in size again, about 30 minutes. Bake until brown. About 20 to 25 minutes.

*REMEMBER, IN BAKING USE MOST OF THE HEAT ON TOP OF THE DUTCH OVEN*

# Pies, Cupcakes, Cookies

Make up your favorite pie and get it ready and in the pie pan. Level your oven over a low heat. Put three rocks or three pieces of rolled-up aluminum foil in the Dutch oven to put the pie on. (This will be like a shelf in your oven to let the heat circulate all around the pie and keep it away from the hot bottom of the oven.) Then put the lid on and add heat to the top.

Cooking time will be about the same as at home in your kitchen, depending on the altitude and heat used, so keep your eye on it.

Cookies and cupcakes can be done the same, just mix up your favorite recipe. Put them on a pan and then put pan and all in the Dutch Oven. My favorite is chocolate chip cookies, even from the mix they are good. They cook in about 10-15 minutes where at home it usually takes about 8-10 minutes.

Use 10 briquets on bottom and 18-24 on top. Use a rack to put pan on or 3 pices of rolled-up aluminum foil.

# White Bread

| | |
|---|---|
| 1 package active dry or 1 cake<br>  compressed yeast<br>½ cup water<br>2 cups milk, scalded<br>2 Tbsp. sugar | 2 Tsp. salt<br>1 Tpsp. shortening<br>6½ to 6¾ cups sifted<br>  enriched flour |

Soften the active dry yeast in warm water (110⁰) or the compressed yeast in lukewarm water (85⁰). Combine the milk, sugar, salt, and shortening. Cool to lukewarm. Add flour; stir well. Add softened yeast; stir. Add flour to make moderately stiff dough.

Turn out on a lightly floured surface; knead till smooth and satiny (about 8 minutes). Shape into ball; place in lightly greased bowl, turning once to grease surface. Cover; let rise in a warm place till double in bulk (about 1½ hours), then punch down. Let it rise again till double in size (about 45 minutes).

Divide into 2 portions. Shape each into a smooth ball; let sit 10 minutes. Shape into loaves; place in 2 greased 9½" x 5¼" x 2¾" loaf pans. Let rise till double, about 1 hour.

If you make a full recipe, you will not have enough room in your Dutch oven for two 9" x 5" loaves. Either use two ovens or cut the recipe to accommodate two 8" x 3" pans.

Bake with 24 to 30 briquets on top and 10 to 12 on the bottom. One hour, 15 minutes baking time is required.

# Zucchini Bread

| | |
|---|---|
| 3 eggs<br>1 cup oil<br>2 cups sugar<br>2 cups flour<br>3 Tsp. vanilla | 2 Tsp. baking powder<br>¼ Tsp. soda<br>3 Tsp. cinnamon<br>2 cups grated raw zucchini<br>1 cup nuts |

Mix together in the order given in a large bowl. Place in two bread pans, 8" x 4". Bake in a Dutch oven with 18 to 20 briquets on top and 8 to 12 on the bottom. Cook for approximately 1 hour and 15 minutes. Test with a toothpick.

These quick bread recipes are ones my wife has used often and they have always been delicious.

If you raise your own zucchini and have more than you can use at harvest, wash the zucchini and grate it on a coarse grater. Measure it into two cup amounts (just enough for a batch of bread). Place it in plastic freezer bags and freeze until needed.

# Banana Nut Bread

| | |
|---|---|
| 5 overripe bananas | ½ Tsp. salt |
| 1 cup sugar | 1 Tsp. baking powder |
| 2 eggs | 1 cup chopped nuts |
| ½ cup shortening | 1 Tsp. baking soda |
| 2 cups flour | |

Mash the bananas and add sugar. Let stand about 15 minutes. Add the shortening and beaten eggs. Sift the flour and measure it. Add all other dry ingredients *except baking soda.* Dissolve the soda in 1 Tbsp. of warm water, then add it to the mixture. Stir only until all ingredients are moistened. Add nuts. Bake in greased loaf pans, 8" x 4". Bake in your Dutch oven with 18 to 20 briquets on top and 8 to 12 on the bottom. Cook for approximately 1 hour and 15 minutes. Test with a toothpick.

Do you ever have bananas become so ripe no one in the family will eat them, yet there aren't enough to make bread? Did you know you can freeze them? Put them in a plastic bowl, adding ripe bananas as they come. When you have enough, let them thaw and use as directed.

# Pumpkin Nut Bread

| | |
|---|---|
| 2 cups sifted flour | 1 cup pumpkin |
| 2 Tsp. baking powder | 1 cup sugar |
| ½ Tsp. soda | ½ cup milk |
| 1 Tsp. salt | 2 eggs |
| 1 Tsp. cinnamon | ½ cup softened butter |
| ½ Tsp. nutmeg | 1 cup chopped pecans |

Sift together the flour, baking powder, soda, salt, and spices. Combine the pumpkin, sugar, milk, and eggs in a mixing bowl. Add the dry ingredients and softened butter; mix until well blended. Stir in the nuts. Spread in a well-greased loaf pan, 9" x 5" x 3". Bake with 18 to 20 briquets on top and 10 to 12 on the bottom. Bake for approximately 1 hour.

# Pizza Crust

My wife got this recipe from her sister and we have enjoyed many pizzas since.

| | |
|---|---|
| 1 yeast cake dissolved in | 3 cups flour |
| 1 cup warm water with 1 Tbsp. | ¾ Tsp. salt |
|   sugar | ½ cup cooking oil |

Mix all the ingredients in together and knead until smooth. Let raise approximately 20 minutes. Separate the dough into two balls and spread out on a greased pizza pan.

Top with anything you desire beginning with tomato sauce. Our favorite pizza is chopped onions, sliced olives, sliced pepperoni, or sausage, sliced mushrooms and lots of mozzarella and sharp cheddar cheese.

Bake with 30 to 36 briquets on top and 8 to 10 briquets on the bottom, for approximately 30 minutes. If you want an extra thick crust, use all the dough on one pizza.

Chapter Ten

# Cooking for Groups

In this section of the book I will give you some tips on cooking in Dutch ovens for a group. I'll suggest some of the meals that work out well for a group, tell how much to cook, recommend how many ovens to use, and suggest how to lay out a cooking area for safety and ease of cooking. After getting the formula down, you can cook anything for a large group that you want.

As a general rule, I first find out how many are going to be eating so I can judge how much food to prepare.

If all adults, I fix ½ pound of meat per person and ½ pount of potatoes and onions per person. If you know their eating habits and they all eat heavily, then cook some extra. Remember that most people, even kids, will eat more Dutch oven food than other food, especially when out camping, so you will have to make a guess. To give you an idea to go by, here is my average guide for pounds to cook:

| | | PEOPLE TO SERVE | | |
| | | 25 | 50 | 100 |
| --- | --- | --- | --- | --- |
| Boneless Brisket | ½ lb. per person | 13 lbs. | 25 lbs. | 50 lbs. |
| Roast w/bone in | 1 lb. per person | 25 lbs. | 50 lbs. | 100 lbs. |
| Beef Short Ribs | 1 lb. per person | 25 lbs. | 50 lbs. | 100 lbs. |
| Pork Spare Ribs | 1 lb. per person | 25 lbs. | 50 lbs. | 100 lbs. |
| Potatoes & Onions | ½ lb. per person | 13 lbs. | 25 lbs. | 50 lbs. |
| (4 parts potatoes, 1 part onions) | | | | |
| Chicken | ½ chicken per person | 13 ch. | 25 ch. | 50 ch. |

For more than 100, add the additional column that applies. For example, for 150 people total the 100 column and the 50 column. This will give you a basis to start with.

Now for how many ovens to use for a group. This chart should be of some help:

| People to Cook For | Ovens Needed 25 | 50 | 100 | Cooking Time | Oven Size |
|---|---|---|---|---|---|
| Potatoes & Onions | 2 | 4 | 6 | ¾ - 1 hr. | 12" |
| " " | 1 | 3 | 5 | ¾ - 1 hr. | 14" |
| Roast, Boneless | 2 | 4 | 6 | 2 - 3 hrs. | 12" |
| " " | 1 | 3 | 5 | 2 - 3 hrs. | 14" |
| Roast w/bone in | 3 | 5 | 7 | 2 - 3 hrs. | 12" |
| " " | 2 | 4 | 6 | 2 - 3 hrs. | 14" |
| Short Ribs or Spare Ribs | 3 | 5 | 7 | 3 hrs. | 12" |
| " " " " | 2 | 4 | 6 | 3 hrs. | 14" |
| Cobblers | 2 | 5 | 7 | ¾ - 1 hr. | 12" |
| " | 2 | 4 | 6 | ¾ - 1 hr. | 14" |
| Chicken | 3 | 5 | 7 | 1 - 1½ hrs. | 12" |
| " | 2 | 4 | 6 | 1 - 1½ hrs. | 14" |

This is only a guide to help you estimate how many ovens to use. If you don't have that many available, use what you have. Use some to hold the meat or ribs in. By cutting down on the heat and stocking it full (but so the lid will still close), you can get by with fewer ovens. It will take longer to cook it, so allow more time for cooking. After one item you are cooking is done and the other is not, you can consolidate it in a few ovens, then cut the heat down for holding until the other food is done, so you can serve it together. (See the note on holding ovens at the end of Group Menu Section.)

As you can see by the chart on how many ovens to use, there is work involved here, so make sure you have some help so you don't have to do it alone or it can be a hard day. By having some good help and doing a little planning, it will be a good day, and the meal at the end will be worth all the work to prepare it.

For a group cookout you should have one person to keep the fire going for the coals (or the feeder fire of briquets, whichever you are using), and then at least two people for the meat dishes and two for the potatoes and onions. If a larger group is being cooked for, you will need more to help in all areas. This will come to you after you have had a few cookouts. Remember, it is better to have more help than you need than not enough help.

This is also a good time to teach someone how to cook in Dutch ovens and give them a chance to see how to do it. Let them help with it so they can be more help next time.

Here is a diagram of how to lay out a group cooking area to keep safe from hot briquets and still have everything as convenient as possible.

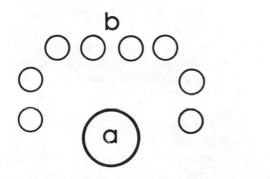

A. Main fire, wood or briquettes (2 feet from nearest cooking fire).
B. Cooking fires as needed (6 inches to 1 foot between each cooking fire).
C. Table for food preparation (6 feet from cooking fires).

It is a good idea to have a table handy to prepare the food on. Even a folding camp table will do. This makes it easier to slice meat and potatoes and to prepare the cobblers. Also, have the main fire or pile of briquets so you can shovel them from it to the individual cooking fires as needed. Make sure you keep adding to the main fire more wood or briquets as needed. Be careful not to get the cooking fires too close to each other. Leave enough space so you don't get burned by one while checking on the one next to it. Try to keep the coals or briquettes under the oven so no one steps on them while cooking and burns their shoes.

Remember, you can stack ovens on top of each other to use less coals or briquets so the heat on top of one will be the bottom heat of the one on top. It saves heat. Since they have to be moved off to check the food, this arrangement works better for the food that takes longer to cook.

Now all this has been discussed, let's use a real test menu so you can see how I do it.

Say 100 people want a brisket of beef dinner. You look at the chart and buy 50 lbs. of boneless brisket, 50 lbs. of potatoes and onions (40 lbs. potatoes, 10 lbs. onions or your combination depending on how well you like onions). Then look at the chart on how many ovens it will take. It will take five 14" ovens to cook the meat and five more 14" ovens to cook the potatoes. You will need 1 pound of bacon per 14" oven for the flavor and grease to cook in. Your shopping list will be: 50 lbs. brisket, 40 lbs. potatoes, 10 lbs. onions, 5 lbs. bacon (bacon is used to flavor the onions and potatoes). This is plus the cobblers that we'll be going into later. I would suggest that someone else should be in charge of the salads, rolls, butter, drink, etc., so that the cooks can concentrate on the cooking.

Now you have the food ready to start, and you know you will need five ovens for meat first so you can start them as soon as the coals are ready. Put them along one side all together so they can be watched. After all the meat is on and cooking, about 1½ hours before you plan to eat, get the five ovens for the potatoes on and the one pound of bacon cut in small serving pieces into each one. While the bacon is cooking, have someone cut up the potatoes and onions so you will be ready when the bacon is crisp. Add the potatoes and onions to the bacon in the ovens. Fill them up so the lid will still close, and so they can be turned over without all falling out of the oven. It will take about one hour to cook the potatoes and onions. Keep an eye on the briquets and meat too. With a little practice, you can have them all done at the same time.

## Holding

The menu for most of the many large groups I have cooked for has been chicken, ribs or roast with potatoes and onion and bacon. But you can fix anything you want to, with the time, ovens, and some good help. It would be a meal to remember. For that reason I think it might be of some help to explain in more detail about holding ovens, and why I use them in cooking for a large group.

No matter what you are cooking, because of the different size of the cuts of meat or chicken and the different heat used on the ovens, all the food you cook will not be done at the same time. You may also have more to cook than you have ovens to hold it.

To start with, when you're browning the roast, chicken or ribs, you only want one layer at a time until all are browned. Only then can you put in extra layers to cook. You can use some of your ovens as browning ovens and some as cooking ovens. After the food is browned, start putting it in the cooking ovens. These cooking ovens will become the holding ovens when the food in them is done the way you want it. Have the holding ovens in their own area and cut the heat down so the food will stay warm but not get over cooked.

The best way to handle the holding ovens is to decide how many you need, then keep them together so you know which are for cooking and which are for holding. Keep the heat low like it should be for holding.

When the food cooking is done, pick the oven up with a hook and move it from the cooking fire to the holding area. Take off the lid and transfer the food to the holding oven. Make sure you don't put too much in the oven or the lid won't close as it should. Return the empty cooking oven to the cooking area so you can start cooking more of whatever needs to be cooked.

Do this with the potatoes and onions too, because when you start out with an ovenfull, by the time they finish cooking they will be down to ½ an ovenfull. So by putting them in a holding oven you have half as many holding ovens as you had cooking ovens. An example is: six ovens, full to start with, will cook down to three when consolidated into three holding ovens.

This is the best way to cook for a large group. By using holding ovens, all the food can be eaten together and it will all still be warm.

I don't want to give you the idea it is too big a job, but it will be work, as you can see. However, with planning ahead and help, you can have a good time doing it and the food is always worth the effort. Remember, nothing worthwhile comes without some effort.

Now that the meat and potatoes are done, you can start serving the food. Consolidate the meat in as few ovens as you can, the potatoes too. When ready to serve the meat and potatoes, have someone dish them out, chow line style. Then, after everybody had had some, those that want to have more can get second helpings.

Now for the cobbler dessert. As soon as the cooks have eaten, it will be time to cook the cobblers. Check your chart and you can see it will take six 14" ovens for 100 people. If you want to try to fix one that everyone likes, fix a variety of them; perhaps 2 apple, 2 cherry, and 2 berry. For each 14" cobbler, it takes 4 cans of filling and one cake mix. So set up your Dutch ovens and get them all lined with aluminum foil, while someone else opens the cans. The cake mixes should be mixed in a separate bowl, one at a time, and poured over the fruit mixture. Doing it one at a time gives the right amount of cake mix to each one. When all are ready, get them on the fire. Look at your watch so you can check them after 20 minutes to see how they are doing. They should cook in 35 to 45 minutes. When they are all done, line the ovens up in a row and get the ice cream out on the end. Serve the cobblers first, then dish up ice cream over it. Serve while warm.

# Chapter Eleven

# Dutch Oven Cooking in Emergencies

I have commented about using the Dutch oven for cooking in the event of a power failure, or gas shortage, etc., in several places of this book. I think it would be good to go more into detail about what you can do if you have to.

As a buffer against any truck strikes or disaster we have a stock of briquets in 20-lb. bags and rotate them so we always have at least 100-lbs. on hand for an emergency. With food on hand, a Dutch oven and briquets, you are ready for whatever comes.

Now I don't want to be a "portrayer of doom," but I believe in applying the message of the Scout motto wherever possible as that motto says "Be Prepared." It is better to be prepared for an emergency than to wish you had prepared when you are in one.

I will give you some ideas of food storage items you can cook in Dutch ovens without too much trouble. It's not as fast as a microwave or regular oven, but with power shut off it can make the difference between having a good hot meal or having to eat sandwiches all the time. I don't know about you, but I get tired of sandwiches after a while. After thinking about it, I hope you agree that with a little help you can eat much better with Dutch oven cooking in any kind of emergency.

Most of the recipes in this book you could use even if the power were to be off for a long period of time and the food in your freezer would spoil if it was not cooked immediately. What a help it would be, then, to have some knowledge about Dutch oven cooking.

Besides that, let me suggest several new items for you to try from your food storage wheat, etc.

# Chile Wheat

Soak the wheat the day before you plan on cooking it. Put 2 cups of wheat in 4 cups of warm water. Put it in a pan to soak it overnight before cooking it the next day. Drain the water off the wheat when adding to the recipe.

| | |
|---|---|
| 2 cups soaked whole wheat (cleaned) | 1 Tsp. garlic powder |
| 2 lbs. ground beef | 4 cups tomato juice |
| 1 large onion | 1 to 2 cups of cheese |
| 1 Tsp. chile powder | salt and pepper |

Mix wheat and tomato juice in your Dutch oven and cook on low heat 3 to 5 hours. After it has been cooking for 3 to 4 hours, mix the meat and onions with the chile powder, garlic powder and salt and pepper. Brown in another oven until good and brown, then combine with other ingredients in one oven. Let simmer on low heat 30 minutes to one hour. Then sprinkle the grated cheese on top. Continue to simmer. Add heat to top of oven to brown cheese. Remove and serve with crackers or fresh baked bread. Serve while warm.

# Dutch Oven Quick Wheat
# Dutch Oven Parched Wheat

Put a thin layer of clean whole wheat in the Dutch oven and sprinkle with 2 to 3 Tbsp. water. Season to taste with seasoned salt, garlic salt, or plain salt. Bake with most of the heat on top until wheat changes color. Stir it often.

You can also try whole wheat cereal or cracked whole wheat cereal. Most recipe books have recipes like this you can use, just keep your eye on the food and you should do fine.

Another good meal you can fix would be homemade bread and some canned soup from storage. If milk is available, use creamed soup with it. If not available, then use soup that needs only water. Bake the bread first as it will take longer. The soup will heat in about ten minutes or less.

For a change, with the canned soup add some elbow macaroni to vegetable beef. With homemade bread cooked in your Dutch oven, it's not a bad meal at all.

For another meal use canned beef soup and add the biscuits to it, then bake in your Dutch oven until the biscuits are brown. It will be ready in about 10 to 15 minutes in a 10" oven (longer if you have to fix more).

With the canned goods you now have on hand, if for any reason you are without power or gas for a while, with a little practice and some knowledge of Dutch oven cooking it might surprise you how well you can provide for your family. I am sure you could think up a lot of meals to fix if you had to. Practice a few meals and be prepared for anything rather than just thinking about it and not being ready if the need does come.

## T.V.P.

Another food storage item we have experimented with is T.V.P. beef-flavored soybeans. After trying several combinations, we found that by mixing no more than half T.V.P. and half ground meat, you couldn't tell it had been added to the meat. It is high in protein and low in cost, so why not try it? We have used it in the meat loaf, burgers, hamburger steak, and chile and it was good in all of them and could sure help stretch your meat when you have to.

When you try it, soak it in warm water about ten minutes, drain and mix with the meat. It might surprise you how good it is.

For a few more ideas of meals you can fix, try these. You can see by all of these suggestions that the only limit to what you can fix will be what food you have on hand and some ideas to get you started. For example: We all have vegetables in our freezer and canned ones on our shelves. You should have some canned meat like beef and gravy, corned beef, tuna fish, Spam, etc. So for starters, cook what meat you have in your Dutch oven as you would in your kitchen, except you will use briquets outside or a Coleman stove, if you have one.

Fry the Spam as in a frying pan. While it is browning, put another oven on and put in some water, as you would if cooking on your kitchen stove. Salt to taste and put in the vegetables you have frozen or canned. You can fix any kind you want.

Now for a couple of things you can do to help it taste better. To meat like Spam add a can of cream of onion or mushroom soup. For vegetables like frozen cauliflower, asparagus, or broccoli, why not add some canned cheese sauce or grate up some cheese to add after the vegetables have cooked.

You do this by draining off any extra water. Cut the heat down on the bottom of the oven, put the cheese on the top of the vegetables, put the lid back on, and then put some heat on top to melt the cheese. It can surely add extra flavor to a vegetable dish and protein too.

You can even fix a vegetable to go with a sandwich you made from bread you baked in your Dutch oven. Suggestions for easy sandwiches are: tuna, ham salad, corn beef, chicken salad, or whatever easy meat you have available.

If you like creamed tuna on toast or creamed beef on toast, use a can of white sauce and cream it as you usually do. While heating it in one oven, make toast by heating up another oven, or just the lid turned over will work well too. Butter the bread on both sides and put it in the oven to toast (a few minutes on each side). The creamed mixture should be ready to pour over the toast. Don't be afraid to try a few things. You may be surprised how well you can eat with a little planning and some knowledge of the Dutch oven. It will surely beat going hungry, or having the food you do have go bad because you don't know how to cook without electricity or gas.

# Chapter Twelve

# Complementary Side Dishes

As much as I enjoy Dutch oven cooking, for a good balanced diet you need other foods too. Before concluding this book, I would like to tell you about a few side dishes we enjoy that will complement the Dutch oven meal with which they're served.

## Special Fruit Salad

*Sauce Mixture:*

⅓ cup sugar                ½ cup pineapple juice
2 Tbsp. flour              1 egg
pinch salt                 1 Tsp. lemon juice

Add all dry ingredients, then add the egg and juices. Combine together and stir. Cook until it thickens.

1 cup Acini Pepe (Ronzone #44)    2½ Tsp. salt
1 quart boiling water              1 Tbsp. oil

Bring water, salt, and oil to boil. Add Acini Pepe to the boiling water. Cook 8 to 10 minutes, then drain and rinse. Pour in the sauce mixture.

Then add:

3-oz. Cool Whip                ¾ cup crushed pineapple
1 11-oz. can mandarin oranges  ⅔ cup small marshmallows
1 11-oz. can pineapple tidbits ½ cup shredded coconut

Make sure the sauce mixture and Acini Pepe are cool before you add the remaining ingredients. If not, the marshmallows and Cool Whip will melt.

# Fresh Fruit Salad Bowl

Cut one watermelon about ⅓ of the way down, the long way of the melon. Take out the pulp to form a bowl and cut the melon in 1" squares. Place these, with other assorted fruit, back into the watermelon bowl. Other fruits that may be used are cantaloup, seedless grapes, strawberries, pineapple, raspberries, and pitted bing cherries. Any combination can be used. This salad is especially good for those counting calories as no dressing is used, just natural juices.

# Potato Salad Supreme

| | |
|---|---|
| 6 medium potatoes | 1 cup mayonnaise |
| 1 medium onion | 1 Tsp. salt |
| 6 eggs | |

Peel and cut potatoes into chunk-size pieces. Place them in salted water to cover. Cook until tender. Hardboil the eggs. While the potatoes are still warm add finely-diced onion. Peel the eggs and slice them into several slices, then add them to the warm mixture. Add mayonnaise and mix well. The salad will have the appearance of whipped potatoes.

This salad can be served while still warm, or cooled and served later.

# INDEX

## A-B

# K-L

# O

# P

# R

## S